3 4028 07544 5032
HARRIS COUNTY PUBLIC LIBRARY

D0848580

· Jaffrey
able
dishes from India,
$35.00
ocn503042015
1st American ed   10/21/2010

ALSO BY MADHUR JAFFREY

An Invitation to Indian Cooking

Madhur Jaffrey's World-of-the-East Vegetarian Cooking

Madhur Jaffrey's Indian Cooking

A Taste of India

Madhur Jaffrey's Cookbook

Madhur Jaffrey's Far Eastern Cookery

A Taste of the Far East

Madhur Jaffrey's Spice Kitchen

Flavours of India

Madhur Jaffrey's World Vegetarian

Step-by-Step Cooking

Quick and Easy Indian Cooking

From Curries to Kebabs

Climbing the Mango Trees

FOR CHILDREN

Seasons of Splendour

Market Days

Robi Dobi:
The Marvellous Adventures of an Indian Elephant

At Home with Madhur Jaffrey

AT HOME WITH

Madhur Jaffrey

Simple, Delectable Dishes from

INDIA, PAKISTAN,

BANGLADESH, & SRI LANKA

PHOTOGRAPHS BY CHRISTOPHER HIRSHEIMER

DECORATIVE DRAWINGS BY MADHUR JAFFREY

ALFRED A. KNOPF   NEW YORK   2010

THIS IS A BORZOI BOOK
PUBLISHED BY ALFRED A. KNOPF

Copyright © 2010 by Madhur Jaffrey

All rights reserved.
Published in the United States by Alfred A. Knopf,
a division of Random House, Inc., New York,
and in Canada by Random House of Canada Limited, Toronto.
www.aaknopf.com

Knopf, Borzoi Books, and the colophon are registered
trademarks of Random House, Inc.

Originally published in different form in Great Britain as
Curry Easy by Ebury Press, an imprint of Ebury Publishing,
the Random House Group Ltd., London.

Photographs by Christopher Hirsheimer.
Illustrations by Madhur Jaffrey were originally published in
An Invitation to Indian Cooking by Madhur Jaffrey,
copyright © 1973 by Madhur Jaffrey (New York: Alfred A. Knopf, Inc.).
They appear here courtesy of Alfred A. Knopf,
a division of Random House, Inc.

Library of Congress Cataloging-in-Publication Data
Jaffrey, Madhur, [date]
At home with Madhur Jaffrey : simple, delectable dishes from India,
Pakistan, Bangladesh, and Sri Lanka / by Madhur Jaffrey.—1st ed.
p. cm.
Includes index.
ISBN 978-0-307-26824-2
1. Cookery, Asian.   2. Cookery—South Asia.   I. Title.
TX724.5.A1J297 2010
641.5950—dc22
2010019678

Manufactured in China
First American Edition

For Sanford

Contents

Introduction

The techniques used in Indian cooking are not any different from those used the world over: roasting, grilling, steaming, frying, stewing, braising, and so on. What gives Indian cuisine its uniqueness, its tingling excitement, and its health-giving properties is the knowledgeable use of spices and seasonings, ancient in its provenance.

It is this very use of spices and seasonings that appears daunting to many approaching Indian cooking for the first time.

My purpose in writing this book is to vanquish that fear, to make Indian dishes as simple and straightforward to prepare as, say, a beef stew, and to hold your hand through the entire process with clear instructions and detailed explanations.

My own cooking has changed over the years. I am often as rushed for time as perhaps you are. I am always asking myself, Is there an easier way to do this? So, over the decades, I have simplified my cooking greatly. I now try to reach real Indian tastes by using simpler methods and fewer steps.

It is these newer recipes that you will find in this book. Just to give you an example: to make a proper curry generally calls for the browning of wet seasonings such as onion, garlic, and ginger, the browning of dry spices like cumin, chilies, and coriander, and the browning of the meat itself. Now I find that if I just marinate the meat with all the spices and seasonings and then bake it, both covered and uncovered, all the browning happens on its own; the curry absorbs the spices and is delicious.

I also searched for recipes that are simple to begin with. India has so many of those. Very often all you require is a little oil, a few whole spices, and the vegetable or fish. Sauté and it is done. No fuss at all. Shrimp, potatoes, peas, they can all be cooked this way.

I have also used a smaller palette of spices. There is still a good range of them. Indian food would not be as magical without them. But these days, going out to look for spices and seasonings is no longer necessary, as all of them are offered by the Web sites of stores located in every country. Yes, your fingers can do the walking! And if you are adding one spice at a certain stage of the cooking, you can just as easily add three or four or six.

Read the recipes thoroughly before starting to cook, as sometimes an overnight marination is required. Also, it is a good idea to have all the preparations done and the spices measured out beforehand, since seasonings may need to go into the cooking pot in quick succession. Sometimes spices need to be ground. I use a coffee grinder reserved for spices, but a mortar and pestle also will do.

The recipes in this book come mainly from India but include the whole family of South Asian nations: India, Pakistan, Bangladesh, and Sri Lanka. Within these pages you will discover a crispy okra salad with slivers of shallots and tomatoes (page 165), spinach and ginger soup perfumed with cloves from Sri Lanka (page 35), tandoori-style striped bass fillet (page 43) from North India, Bengali-style grilled masala salmon (page 46), Pakistani stir-fried chicken breast with black pepper and green chilies (page 80), grilled lamb chops (page 119), pan-grilled zucchini (page 173), and green lentils with green beans and cilantro (page 191), both modern dishes, and the wonderful pudding, tapioca pearl *kheer* (page 272) from my mother's kitchen. I love them all, and you can make them with ease.

For most Indians, the center of the meal is the starch, usually rice or bread or, in some cases, both. Then there are all the things you eat with it. There is meat or fish (at banquets both may be served), one or two vegetables, some kind of *dal* (dried beans or split peas), some form of yogurt, a salad, and a selection of pickles and chutneys. Vegetarians would, of course, leave out the meat or fish. I have offered serving suggestions with some of the main dishes, but feel free to make your own choice. I have not always added the *dal*s and relishes to these suggestions, but remember, they are the constants, present at most full meals. I have used the word *dal* frequently in this book. Even though *dal* is, technically, a dried split pea, the word is commonly used for all legumes—dried beans and split peas. When Indians talk about having dined, they say, "I have eaten my *dal bhat* [*dal* and rice] or *dal roti* [*dal* and *roti*]. *Dal* is a very important part of the meal.

You may also serve some of the dishes in this book with Western accompaniments or use these dishes as accompaniments to Western foods. For example, Ground Turkey with Hyderabadi Seasonings (page 102) may be served with hot corn tortillas and a salsa, and Pakistani-Style Grilled Lamb Chops (page 119) may be served with boiled potatoes and sautéed spinach. Do what is easy and comfortable.

Appetizers, Snacks, and Soups

Indians do not really eat an appetizer course. What happens in most homes is that an announcement is made that lunch or dinner is ready. Everyone goes first to wash their hands and then to take their places at the table—or the floor, if that is where the food is to be consumed. Most of the food appears at the same time—the meats, the vegetables, the rice or breads, the legumes, the yogurt relishes, the salads, the pickles and chutneys. At the end of the meal there is fresh fruit. For a special occasion, there may even be a dessert.

There are some Indian communities, however, that do eat their meals in courses: at banquets, the Bohra Muslims of Gujarat alternate between salty and sweet dishes and actually start with a pinch of salt; the Bengalis of East India and the Tamils of the south are known to have each of their courses with rice. At festive dinners Bengalis might start with rice and a crisp fritter, whereas a Tamil might begin his everyday meal with rice, some *ghee* (clarified butter), and a prayer.

When Indian restaurants began opening up around the world in the 1950s, they were modeled on Western ones, and it was thought that some form of starter was needed. So the restaurateurs dug into India's vast repertoire of snack foods, colonial soups, and the world of kebabs and tandoori meats and came up with, voilà, appetizers. Housewives entertaining at home—and the one writing this book must be included— have continued along the same merry path, adapting whatever we possibly could to fit into this new, Western, category of food.

Some of the dishes in this chapter may be served with drinks—the *pappadom*s, the spicy popcorn, the nuts, the fried whitebait, and the kebabs. The cheese toast may be served with tea. The mushrooms and eggplant dishes are real appetizer courses, as are all the soups.

Is it a part of India's culinary tradition to offer soup? Yes and no. Well, that is India for you. You can never get a simple answer.

In India's Muslim culinary tradition, there is *aab gosht,* meat broth, which is served at the start of a meal. (I was once at a grand Hyderabadi banquet where we were offered this soup in antique English teacups while we were still in the drawing room.) Then, during our colonial period, the British introduced us to so many soups that we began to suspect that these watery concoctions were what sustained the Empire and that the British would just wither away without them. There was tomato soup, which remains a favorite, but also soups made with cauliflower, spinach, peas, and legumes. Of course, when Indians made these dishes in their homes, they were Indianized—with some ginger here, some cloves and green chilies there. Then there is a third category, India's ancient soupy dishes that are served as part of the main meal but are quite amenable to being served as a first course. There is *rasam,* the "pepper water" of Tamil Nadu, from which the British concocted mulligatawny soup; the *saar*s of Maharashtra, which are often spiced fruit purees, sometimes made with the addition of coconut milk; and the various *kadhi*s of northern and western India, which have as their base beaten yogurt thickened with chickpea flour. And who can forget the magnificent *dal dhokli* of Gujarat, a soupy, spicy mix of split peas and tomatoes with some pappardelle-type homemade pasta ribbons floating around in it?

Pappadoms or Papar/Papad

Known by different names in the north and south of India, these crisp wafers are an essential part of Indian cuisine, as "something with a crunch" completes a meal in many parts of India. Known as *pappadoms* in the south and *papar/papad* in the north, they are generally made out of a split-pea dough that is rolled out into paper-thin round discs and dried in the sun (the desert areas of India are ideal for this). The ones I like best are made of *urad dal* (page 284) and flavored with peppercorns. You buy them from Indian grocers, but they still need cooking.

The traditional way was to fry them in very hot oil for a few seconds, which made them expand into marvelous Frank Gehry shapes. Now I just cook them in the microwave oven. They do not expand as much, but they still take on Zaha Hadid shapes and are wonderfully crunchy without being oily.

Make as many *pappadoms* as you wish, and serve them with drinks or as part of a meal.

MAKES 1

1 pappadom/papar/papad

Break the *pappadom* into two halves. Put a paper towel into the microwave oven and place the *pappadom* on top with straight edges facing outward. Microwave for 40–60 seconds, depending upon the strength of your oven.

Seasoned Radishes

I love these radishes and cannot stop eating them. I like to serve them with drinks, but you may serve them with grilled meats or as a relish with a meal.

SERVES 4

1 dozen medium radishes
½ teaspoon salt

¼ teaspoon cayenne pepper
1 tablespoon red wine vinegar

Remove the green radish tops and their tails, wash well, and then cut each radish in half lengthwise. Combine the radishes with the salt, cayenne, and vinegar in a small bowl, mix well, and set aside for 3 hours, tossing every now and then. Drain the radishes and serve.

Spiced Roasted Cashews

When I was growing up in Delhi, my mother regularly deep-fried cashews for us in a *karhai* (wok). She would scoop the nuts up from the hot oil with a slotted spoon and leave them to drain on a crisp sheet of brown paper—the same kind she used to cover our schoolbooks. My father ate them with his evening whisky-and-soda and the rest of us nibbled on them with our soft drinks. I have now taken to roasting the cashews instead. Nothing could be easier.

MAKES 1 CUP AND SERVES 6–8 WITH DRINKS

1 cup (5½ ounces) raw cashews
1 teaspoon olive or canola oil
½ teaspoon salt

½ teaspoon ground cumin seeds
½ teaspoon cayenne pepper

Preheat oven to 350°F.

Line a small baking tray with foil and spread the cashews out in a single layer. Dribble the oil over them and toss them well so the oil clings to them like a film. Sprinkle the salt, cumin, and cayenne over them and toss thoroughly again to mix. Place in the center of the oven and bake for 12–15 minutes, tossing and mixing every 4–5 minutes. Leave to cool off and firm up before serving.

Roasted Almonds with Black Pepper

Black pepper is native to India. Long before India had red chilies to make foods hot, it relied on black pepper. This recipe harks back to a period that is still part of India's present.

MAKES 1 CUP AND SERVES 6–8 WITH DRINKS

1 cup (5¼ ounces) whole blanched
   almonds
1 teaspoon olive or canola oil
½ teaspoon salt

½ teaspoon ground cumin seeds
Freshly ground black pepper, about
   ½ teaspoon

Preheat oven to 350°F.

Line a small baking tray with foil and spread the almonds out in a single layer. Dribble the oil over them and toss them well so the oil clings to them like a film. Sprinkle the salt, cumin, and black pepper over them and toss thoroughly again to mix. Place in the center of the oven and bake for 12–15 minutes, tossing and mixing every 4–5 minutes. Leave to cool off and firm up before serving.

Perfumed Almonds

Almonds are considered brain food in India. They were always given to us in the morning, especially before exams, after they had been soaked overnight and then peeled. Each one of us got seven almonds—don't ask me why. So here is a delicious, lightly perfumed morning dose for two people. The soaking makes them taste a bit like green almonds. The perfume is an added bonus. You may serve them with drinks. I often offer dinner guests a few of these almonds just before I serve dessert and coffee.

14 ALMONDS

14 whole almonds with skin
5 cardamom pods
1 tablespoon sugar

Put the almonds, cardamom pods, and sugar in a small bowl. Pour 1 cup of boiling water over the top, stir, and leave to soak for 12 hours. Refrigerate if leaving longer. Remove from the water, peel, and serve.

Spicy Popcorn

You can make this with store-bought popcorn (you will need about 4½ quarts), but it is much more fun to pop the corn and season it yourself. If you have your own method of popping corn, do use it. My method is given below.

MAKES ABOUT 4½ QUARTS

5 tablespoons olive or canola oil
1 cup popping corn
1/16 teaspoon ground asafetida (optional)
1½ teaspoons brown mustard seeds
3 tablespoons beige sesame seeds

½ teaspoon ground turmeric
2 teaspoons salt
2 teaspoons fine sugar
½ teaspoon cayenne pepper
1/6 teaspoon ground cloves
1/16 teaspoon ground cinnamon

TO POP THE CORN: Put 3 tablespoons of the oil in a large pot and set on medium-high heat. When hot, put in just a small fistful of the measured popcorn and cover. You will hear the corn popping. Let the popping continue for a few seconds. When most of it is done, remove the pot to the side and leave covered, for exactly 30 seconds (you can count it out). Put the pan back on the heat and add all the remaining popcorn. Cover. Shake. After 3 seconds, turn the heat down to medium. Shake the pot as the corn pops. When all the popping is done, turn off the heat.

Put the remaining 2 tablespoons of oil in a small frying pan and set on medium-high heat. When hot, put in the asafetida, then the mustard seeds, then the sesame seeds. As soon as the seeds start to pop, a matter of seconds, take the pan off the heat and add the turmeric. Stir. Empty the contents of the pan over the popcorn. Add the remaining ingredients and toss thoroughly.

Chickpeas for Nibbling

There is nothing like sitting down for an evening drink with these chickpeas by one's side. Since they come out of a can, no hard work is involved. I like to use organic canned chickpeas, but any kind will do. If you have access to an Indian grocer, do sprinkle the chickpeas with some *chaat masala* at the end. It gives them an extra spiciness. But this is not essential. These are best eaten the day they are made.

SERVES 4 WITH DRINKS

One 15-ounce can of chickpeas (sometimes labeled 425g)
1 teaspoon ground cumin seeds
1 teaspoon ground coriander seeds
¼ teaspoon ground cayenne pepper
½–¾ teaspoon salt

1 tablespoon chickpea flour or plain white flour
1½ tablespoons olive or canola oil, plus more for greasing the baking tray
¼ teaspoon *chaat masala* (optional)

Preheat the oven to 400°F.

Drain the chickpeas and then dry them off thoroughly with several changes of paper towels. Put them in a bowl and add the cumin, coriander, cayenne, and salt. Toss to mix. Add the chickpea or white flour and toss again. Add the oil and toss to mix well. Grease a small baking tray (7" × 10" is ideal) and empty the chickpeas into it, spreading them out evenly. Bake 15 minutes. Stir the chickpeas around and bake another 10–15 minutes. Sprinkle the *chaat masala* over the top if desired and toss.

Cheese Toast

I love cheese toast the way it is done in India—with some chopped fresh green chilies and cilantro thrown in. We like to serve it with tea, as we seem to love the combination of spicy snacks and very hot tea! You can use any white bread (or brown, if you prefer), any cheese you like (I happen to like sharp cheddar), and the chilies could be fresh green ones (about ¼ teaspoon, well chopped) but the pickled Greek ones are fine too, and, as I always have them on hand in my refrigerator and I like the tartness they provide, I use them instead. Some Anglo-Indian recipes have the yolks of hard-boiled eggs mixed with mustard spread inside the sandwich as well.

I make my sandwich in a frying pan, but a panini press, if you have one of those, would work too.

SERVES 1

2 slices of bread
2 thin slices of cheese (sized to fit the bread)

5–6 rings of pickled hot Greek peppers, drained and patted dry
1 teaspoon very finely chopped cilantro
1 tablespoon butter, melted, or olive oil

Put one slice of cheese over one slice of bread, making sure to cover it completely. Spread the pepper rings on top evenly. Sprinkle the cilantro over that. Now cover with the second slice of cheese and then the second slice of bread and press down.

Brush a small, heavy frying pan with half the butter or oil and set on medium-high heat. When hot, put down the sandwich, pressing down on it. Cook until golden brown, still pressing down with a spatula. Then brush the top of the sandwich with the remaining butter or oil, flip the sandwich over, and brown the second side, pressing down again. Cut it in half, if you like, and serve immediately.

Shrimp and Onion Fritters

Known as *bhajia, bhaja, pakora,* and many other names in different parts of India, fritters are an integral part of every single local cuisine in the nation. The flour that is generally used is the protein-rich chickpea flour (though sometimes rice flour is mixed in for extra crunch). That is the constant. After that, anything can be "frittered"—leaves, roots, fish, roe, vegetables, you take your pick. The batter can be thick or thin, spicy or mild, you take your pick again. Most fritters are served with chutneys. Might I suggest Fresh Green Chutney, page 245, or Peshawari Red Pepper Chutney, page 243, here, but, if you do not have time, bottled tomato ketchup or a last-minute squeeze of lime juice will suffice.

In India and Pakistan, fritters are eaten as a snack, with chutneys and tea. In Bangladesh, they can be the first course at a meal, served with rice. In the West, they have acquired another life altogether: they are served as an appetizer in restaurants and with drinks at catered parties.

Ideally, these fritters, rather like French fries, are best eaten as soon as they come out of the frying pan. If that is not possible, make them ahead of time and reheat them in a medium oven for 10 minutes.

MAKES ABOUT 28 FRITTERS AND COULD SERVE 4–6

1 cup chickpea flour (also sold as gram flour or *besan*)
½ teaspoon baking soda
¾ teaspoon salt
Freshly ground black pepper
½–¾ teaspoon cayenne pepper
1 teaspoon ground cumin
2 tablespoons very finely chopped red onions or shallots

2 tablespoons very finely chopped cilantro
½ pound shrimp (6–7 ounces), peeled, deveined, and cut crossways into ⅓-inch pieces
Oil for frying, enough to have ¾–1 inch in a frying pan

Sift the chickpea flour, baking soda, and salt into a bowl. Very slowly add about ½ cup water to get a thick batter of droppable consistency. Keep mixing to get rid of all lumps. Add the black pepper, cayenne, and cumin. Stir to mix well. Now add the onion or shallots, cilantro, and shrimp. Stir to mix.

Put the oil in a frying pan and set on medium heat. Give it plenty of time to heat up. Line a baking tray with paper towels. When the oil is hot (a small piece of batter should sizzle if dropped in), pick up 1 heaping teaspoon of the batter and release it into the hot oil with the help of another teaspoon. Quickly put in enough fritters to use up half the batter. Stir and fry for 6–7 minutes or until the fritters are a reddish gold. Remove with a slotted spoon and spread on the paper towels. Make a second batch the same way as you made the first. Serve hot.

Stir-Fried Spicy Mushrooms

I often offer these as an appetizer. I serve them just the way they are, but you could also serve them on toasted slices of Italian bread or just buttered toast.

SERVES 4

5 tablespoons olive oil

½ teaspoon whole brown mustard seeds

¼ teaspoon whole fennel seeds

15 fresh curry leaves or 10 fresh basil leaves, torn up

1 pound cremini or plain white medium-sized mushrooms, cut lengthwise into ¼-inch-thick slices

1 clove garlic, sliced

Salt

⅛ teaspoon cayenne pepper

2–3 teaspoons lime or lemon juice

1–2 tablespoons finely chopped cilantro or parsley

Put the oil in a large frying pan and set over medium-high heat. When hot, drop in the mustard seeds. As soon as the mustard seeds start to pop, a matter of seconds, put in the fennel seeds and curry leaves. A few seconds later, add the mushrooms and garlic. Stir and fry until the liquid begins to ooze out from the mushrooms, about 2 minutes. Now add about ⅓–½ teaspoon salt (taste as you go), the cayenne, and the lime juice. Stir for a minute. Taste for balance of flavors. Add the cilantro, stir, and turn off the heat. Serve warm or at room temperature.

Grilled Eggplant Slices with Yogurt Sauce

Here you simply marinate eggplant slices in a spicy dressing and then grill them. When serving (hot or cold), spoon a dollop of yogurt seasoned with fresh mint on the top. It is cool and refreshing.

SERVES 4–6

FOR THE MARINADE

2 tablespoons red wine vinegar
1 tablespoon Dijon mustard
1½ tablespoons sugar
1½ teaspoons salt
2 tablespoons Tabasco Sauce
2 tablespoons finely chopped, peeled
  fresh ginger
1 tablespoon ground cumin seeds
1 tablespoon finely chopped garlic
4 tablespoons tomato juice (canned will
  do) or chopped-up tomatoes
4 tablespoons chopped fresh cilantro
2 tablespoons olive or canola oil

YOU ALSO NEED

One large, 1¼-pound eggplant
⅛ teaspoon salt
⅛ teaspoon cayenne pepper
4–5 leaves fresh mint, finely chopped
½ cup plain yogurt

Put all the ingredients for the marinade into a blender and blend until smooth. Pour into a large bowl.

Cut the eggplant crossways into ½-inch-thick, round slices and add to the bowl with the marinade. Toss to coat slices with the marinade. Cover and refrigerate overnight, turning the eggplant pieces over a few times whenever it is convenient.

Heat the broiler. Lift the slices out of the bowl, leaving a light coating of the marinade on them, and lay them in a single layer in a broiling tray. Broil 4–5 inches from the heat for 7–8 minutes a side, moving the slices around so they brown evenly.

Add the salt, cayenne, and mint to the yogurt and mix.

When serving, put a dollop of yogurt on top of each eggplant slice.

Eggplant with Fennel and Cumin

Although Indians do not eat appetizer courses as such, there are many Indian dishes that can be served as a first course. This eggplant dish is one of them. I often serve it that way, with a slice of French bread on the side and some Pinot Grigio to polish it off. You can, of course, also serve it as the vegetable dish with the main course. (I love it with the Tandoori-Style Duck Breasts, page 103.)

SERVES 4–6

One medium-sized eggplant, about 1 pound
6 tablespoons olive or corn oil
1 medium onion, cut into $\frac{1}{4}$-inch-thick half rings
$\frac{1}{2}$ teaspoon whole cumin seeds

$\frac{1}{2}$ teaspoon whole fennel seeds
$\frac{1}{2}$ cup tomato puree
1 teaspoon salt
1 teaspoon sugar
$\frac{1}{4}$ teaspoon cayenne pepper

Cut the eggplant lengthways into 3 slabs. Now cut the slabs into chunky segments that are about 2" × $1\frac{1}{4}$" × $1\frac{1}{4}$".

Pour the oil into a large frying pan or sauté pan and set over medium-high heat. When hot, put in the onions, the cumin, the fennel, and the eggplant. Stir and fry for about 5 minutes or until the onions just start to brown. Add the tomato puree, salt, sugar, cayenne, and $1\frac{1}{4}$ cups water. Bring to a boil. Cover, turn heat to low, and simmer gently, turning the eggplant pieces over now and then, until they are really tender, about 30–35 minutes.

OVERLEAF, LEFT TO RIGHT: *Grilled Eggplant Slices with Yogurt Sauce, Shrimp with Garlic and Chilies, and Baked Pâté-Kebabs*

Stir-Fried Whole Peas in Their Pods

Here is a dish that, as far as I know, was only served in India by my own family. My mother made it; my grandmother made it. It was made only when peas were young and fresh. Even Indians (from other families and from other parts of India) who have dined with us in the pea season are surprised by it.

It requires whole, fresh peas in their pods. I grow my own peas, and this is the first dish I make with them when they are ready for picking. You have to eat the peas rather like artichoke leaves: you put the whole pea pod in your mouth, holding on to it by its stem end, clench your teeth, and pull. What you get to eat are not just the peas themselves but also the softened outsides of the shells. You discard the fibrous bits after getting all the goodness out of them.

We ate this as a snack or at teatime, but I have taken to serving it as a first course.

SERVES 4

2 tablespoons olive or canola oil
$\frac{1}{8}$ teaspoon ground asafetida
$\frac{1}{2}$ teaspoon whole cumin seeds
$1\frac{1}{4}$ pounds fresh whole peas in their
    pods, washed, but with their little
    stems attached

$\frac{1}{4}$ teaspoon salt
$\frac{1}{4}$ teaspoon cayenne pepper
1 teaspoon lemon juice

Put the oil in a wok, *karhai,* or large sauté pan and set on medium-high heat. When hot, put in the asafetida and cumin seeds. Let the cumin seeds sizzle for 5 seconds. Put in the peas, salt, and cayenne. Stir for a minute and add 4 tablespoons water. Cover, turn heat to low, and cook about 10 minutes or until peas are cooked through. Remove cover, add the lemon juice, and stir until all liquid is absorbed. Serve hot or at room temperature.

Fried Whitebait, the Sri Lankan Way

There is nothing quite like sitting at a table by the beach, toes buried in the hot sand, eating these crisp whitebait with a glass of whisky in hand. At least, that is how I love them, but I have also been offered whitebait at a Sri Lankan tea, along with cakes and sandwiches. They were delightful then too. I love to serve them as a first course.

To get the fish nice and crisp, they need to be fried twice. The first frying can be done ahead of time, but the second needs to be done just before eating. They may be served just the way they are or with a dipping *sambol* such as Sri Lankan Coconut Sambol, page 246, or Sri Lankan Cooked Coconut Chutney, page 247.

SERVES 4

9 ounces whitebait

¼ teaspoon salt

Freshly ground black pepper

¾ teaspoon cayenne pepper

2 teaspoons lemon juice

Olive or canola oil for deep-frying

1 cup white flour

Wash the whitebait well and then put them in a strainer to drain thoroughly. Using paper towels, pat them as dry as you can. Put them in a bowl. Add the salt, pepper, cayenne, and lemon juice. Toss to mix and leave 15 minutes.

Put the oil in a wok, *karhai,* or other pan for deep-frying. You need about 2 inches. Set on medium-low heat. Let the oil heat for 4–5 minutes. Meanwhile, spread the flour out in a large plate. Lay a batch of fish singly on the flour. Roll in the flour. Remove and put to one side. Do all the fish this way. Now lift up all the fish (leaving all the flour behind) and put them in a clean sieve. Shake off all extra flour. When the oil is hot, fry the fish in several batches, allowing about a minute for each batch. Remove with a slotted spoon and spread on a baking tray lined with paper towels. Turn off the heat.

Just before eating, heat the oil again on medium-high heat. When very hot, fry the fish in batches again, allowing 3–4 minutes per batch or until fish are golden and crisp. Drain on paper towels and serve hot.

Shrimp with Garlic and Chilies

This is easily one of my favorite first courses for dinner parties, one that I have served repeatedly over the years. Most of the work—and there is very little of it—can be done in advance, and the last-minute stir-frying, which is the ideal way to cook this, takes just a few minutes. If you wish to do the entire cooking in advance, you may, just remember to reheat the shrimp over a low flame. I have even served this dish with drinks. I just stick a toothpick in each shrimp and hand out napkins!

If you cannot find fresh curry leaves, tear up 10 fresh basil leaves and use them instead.

SERVES 4

12 raw jumbo or about 16 medium shrimp, peeled and deveined
1/8–1/4 teaspoon cayenne pepper, or to taste
Freshly ground black pepper
1/4 teaspoon salt
1 teaspoon finely chopped fresh hot green chilies

2 tablespoons olive, canola, or peanut oil
1/2 teaspoon whole brown or yellow mustard seeds
1 large clove garlic, finely chopped
15 fresh curry leaves
5 tablespoons grated tomato (see page 289)

Wash the shrimp well. Leave in a strainer for a while and then pat dry. Put in a bowl. Add the cayenne, pepper, salt, and green chilies. Mix well. The shrimp may be covered and refrigerated until needed.

Put the oil in a wok, *karhai,* or frying pan and set over medium-high heat. When hot, put in the mustard seeds. As soon as the mustard seeds begin to pop, a matter of seconds, add the garlic and stir once or twice. Quickly add the shrimp and curry leaves. Stir a few times. Add the grated tomato and stir again a few times. Turn the heat down to medium low and let the shrimp cook gently, stirring as you do so, until they just turn opaque, a matter of 2 or 3 minutes. Serve immediately.

Baked Pâté-Kebabs

Before cooking, the meat-spice mixture requires a rest in the refrigerator to bring all the flavors together and to give the kebabs their requisite melt-in-the-mouth tenderness. If you cannot get a baking pan of just this size, something a bit smaller or a bit larger will do. (You could also use a 6-inch-square cake tin and cut the kebabs into rectangles—in which case, bake for only 30 minutes.) Serve these pâté-like kebabs with drinks, offering flatbread pieces or crackers to eat them with, or serve them as part of a meal with vegetables or salads. They need an accompanying chutney, such as the Peshawari Red Pepper Chutney, page 243, or the Bengali-Style Tomato Chutney, page 244.

SERVES 8 AS AN APPETIZER, 4 AS A MAIN COURSE

1 pound ground turkey (an equal mixture of dark and light meat is best)

2 tablespoons finely chopped fresh mint

2 tablespoons finely chopped cilantro

2–3 cloves garlic, put through a garlic press

$\frac{3}{4}$–1 teaspoon cayenne pepper, or to taste

4 teaspoons plain yogurt

1 teaspoon salt

$1\frac{1}{2}$ teaspoons store-bought *garam masala*

1 teaspoon ground coriander

4 tablespoons very finely chopped onions

1 egg, lightly beaten

Combine the turkey, mint, cilantro, garlic, cayenne, yogurt, salt, *garam masala,* coriander, and 3 tablespoons of the onions in a bowl. Mix well. Add the egg and mix again. Cover with plastic wrap and refrigerate overnight or at least 4–6 hours.

Preheat oven to 350°F.

Pat the meat firmly into a loaf pan measuring about $3\frac{1}{2}$" × $7\frac{1}{2}$" × $2\frac{1}{2}$". Scatter the remaining 1 tablespoon onions over the top and lightly press them in. Bake 40 minutes. Place under a broiler/grill briefly until the top is just browned. Unmold, with the onion side on top. You may cut into slices or squares and serve or put the loaf out like a pâté and let people help themselves.

Cold Cucumber Soup

I love to make this soup in the summer, when my garden (or the local farmers market) is bursting with cucumbers and tomatoes and the weather is balmy.

The first time I had this soup, or a version of it, was in the Maldives, at the Cocoa Island resort on the South Male Atoll, just southwest of India. For the soup, the chef, Stana Johnson, had combined South Indian seasonings and the notion of North India's favorite cucumber *raita,* a yogurt relish, to fashion a light summery, cooling soup. I remember sitting in an airy pavilion, the calm blue sea on two sides of me, balmy breezes blowing past, sipping the soup a tablespoon at a time, and thinking, "This is what heaven must be like."

While the flavors were easy on the tongue, the soup was complicated to make. I have spent two years simplifying it, trying to retain its essence while cutting down on all the steps a large-staffed restaurant can do with ease. I like to serve the soup with a dollop of Yogurt Rice, page 26 or 217, right in its center. This is not essential. Just a light sprinkling of diced cucumbers and diced cherry tomatoes will do. But do try it once with the Yogurt Rice as well as the sprinkling of cucumbers and tomatoes. (You do not actually have to make the full Yogurt Rice recipe. A very quick version, made with leftover rice, follows.)

SERVES 6–8

2 tablespoons olive or canola oil

2 tablespoons *urad dal* (or yellow split peas)

1 tablespoon whole brown or yellow mustard seeds

2 dried hot red chilies

15 fresh curry leaves, if available, or 6 basil leaves, torn up

4 cups chicken stock

Cucumber, enough to get 3 cups after peeling and blending, plus some finely diced cucumber for garnishing

¾ teaspoon salt, or to taste

2 cups plain yogurt

8 cherry tomatoes, cut into ¼-inch dice, for garnishing

Put the oil in a small pan and set over medium-high heat. When very hot, put in the *dal* or split peas. As soon as the *dal* takes on a hint of color, add the mustard seeds and chilies. As soon as the mustard seeds pop, a matter of seconds, throw in the curry leaves and quickly pour in the chicken stock. Bring to a boil. Turn heat down to medium low and simmer, uncovered, for about 15 minutes or until the stock is reduced to 3 cups. Set aside for 3 hours or overnight in the refrigerator, allowing the stock to chill and get infused with the seasonings. Strain.

Peel and roughly dice the cucumber. Put in a blender along with ½ cup of the strained broth. Blend finely.

Put the salt and yogurt in a large bowl and whisk lightly so you have a smooth mixture. Slowly whisk in the remaining chicken stock and cucumber mixture. Taste for salt and then refrigerate until needed.

TO SERVE: Stir the soup well, as it tends to separate, and ladle into soup bowls. Sprinkle the diced cucumbers and diced tomatoes over the top and serve.

Quick Yogurt-Rice Garnish for Soups

The French drop a dollop of spicy, garlicky rouille in the center of fish soups. It perks them up. Well, this is its Indian incarnation, a quick version of the southern Yogurt Rice, perfect for placing in the center of not only the preceding Cold Cucumber Soup, but all manner of bean and split pea soups.

I like to serve the soups in old-fashioned soup plates, which are shallower than soup bowls. This way the dollop of garnish stands up and is not drowned.

MAKES ENOUGH GARNISH FOR 6–8 SERVINGS

1 cup cooked rice
$\frac{1}{4}$ cup cold milk
$\frac{1}{4}$ cup plain yogurt, lightly beaten
Salt
Freshly ground pepper
2 teaspoons olive or canola oil

$\frac{1}{2}$ teaspoon whole black or yellow
    mustard seeds
10 fresh curry leaves, if available, or
    5 basil leaves, torn up
$\frac{1}{8}$ teaspoon cayenne pepper

Sprinkle the rice with about 2 tablespoons of water and heat through, covered, either in a microwave oven for a minute or in a small pan. While still hot, add the milk first and then the yogurt. Mix. Sprinkle lightly with salt and pepper, checking to make sure it is properly seasoned.

Put the oil in a small pan and set over medium-high heat. When very hot, put in the mustard seeds. As soon as the seeds begin to pop, a matter of seconds, put in the curry leaves and then the cayenne. Now pour this mixture over the yogurt rice. Stir to mix.

Put a generous dollop in the center of each soup plate.

Peshawari Broth with Mushrooms and Fish

Here is a soup that I had in Pakistan's most famous northwestern city, Peshawar. Many of the grander Muslim families, in both India and Pakistan, offer some form of *aab gosht,* or meat broth, at the start of a meal. Sometimes it comes in cups even before one is seated and requires just sipping. This is a variation of that and requires a spoon. What I was offered on a rather cold day was a steaming bowl of well-seasoned goat broth in which floated oyster mushrooms and slices of river fish. It was so delicious that I decided to come up with a version myself. I have used beef stock, though lamb stock would do as well. If you cannot get fresh oyster mushrooms, use the canned ones, sold by all Chinese grocers, or canned straw mushrooms. Just drain them and rinse them out.

SERVES 4

5¼ cups beef broth/stock
½ teaspoon whole cumin seeds
½ teaspoon whole fennel seeds
1 tablespoon whole coriander seeds
6 cardamom pods
6 whole cloves
½ teaspoon whole black peppercorns
Salt
1 tablespoon olive or canola oil
4 ounces fresh oyster mushrooms, broken apart into 1½-inch pieces

1 fresh green bird's-eye chili, or about ⅛ teaspoon of any fresh hot green chili, finely chopped
½ pound fillet of any white fish, such as flounder, without skin, cut into 1" x 2" pieces and sprinkled lightly with salt on both sides
4 tablespoons chopped cilantro

Put the broth, cumin seeds, fennel seeds, coriander seeds, cardamom, cloves, and peppercorns in a medium pan and bring to a boil. Cover, turn heat to low, and simmer very gently for 20 minutes. Strain, then pour strained broth back into the same pan. Check the salt and make adjustments, if needed.

Pour the oil into a nonstick frying pan and set on medium-high heat. When hot, put in the mushrooms and green chili. Stir and sauté for about 2 minutes or until the mushrooms have softened. Salt lightly and stir. Transfer the contents of the frying pan to the pan with the broth.

Just before eating, bring the broth to a boil. Slip in the fish pieces, turning the heat to low. When the fish pieces turn opaque and the broth is simmering, the soup is ready. Sprinkle in the cilantro, stir once, and serve.

Chicken Mulligatawny Soup

Here is a soup of colonial, British-Indian origin, born in the early days of the Raj and a favorite among the dwindling mixed-race Anglo-Indian community of India. All the ingredients and seasonings are completely Indian. It is just the way it is served (in a soup plate) and eaten (with a soup spoon) that is British.

This soup may be served at the start of a meal, but it may also be offered as the main course for a Sunday lunch, the way the Anglo-Indians do. At such times, plain rice is served on the side, with diners adding as much as is desired to their soup plates, a little at a time so as not to solidify the soup in one go. I like to give my guests individual bowls of rice so that a single large bowl of rice does not have to move around the table like a whirling dervish.

SERVES 4

1 pound boneless, skinless chicken thighs (about 3 medium thighs), cut into $\frac{1}{2}$-inch pieces

A scant $\frac{1}{2}$ teaspoon salt

Freshly ground black pepper

1 teaspoon finely grated peeled fresh ginger

3 cloves garlic, crushed to a pulp in a garlic press

$1\frac{1}{2}$ teaspoons ground coriander

1 teaspoon ground cumin

$\frac{1}{4}$ teaspoon cayenne pepper

$\frac{1}{4}$ teaspoon ground turmeric

1 teaspoon hot curry powder

$\frac{1}{4}$ cup olive or canola oil

7 tablespoons chickpea flour, sifted

6 cups chicken stock

3 tablespoons lemon juice

Toss the chicken, salt, pepper, ginger, garlic, coriander, cumin, cayenne, turmeric, and curry powder in a bowl. Mix well, cover, and set aside for 30 minutes to 8 hours, refrigerating if needed.

Pour the oil into a pan large enough to hold the stock easily and set over medium-high heat. When hot, drop in all the chicken. Stir and fry for 3–4 minutes or until the chicken turns white. Add the sifted chickpea flour and continue to stir and fry for about 2 minutes. Slowly add the chicken stock and ½ cup water, stirring from the bottom to collect whatever is stuck down there. Bring to a boil. Cover, turn heat to low, and simmer gently for 20 minutes, stirring now and then. Taste for salt, adding some if your stock was unsalted. Add the lemon juice and stir it in.

Okra–Swiss Chard Soup

This soup, mellowed with coconut milk, is as delicious as it is surprising in its final blend of silken textures.

SERVES 6

3 tablespoons olive or canola oil

1 medium onion, chopped

1 medium carrot, peeled and chopped

4 ounces (about 25) green beans, trimmed and coarsely cut up

25 smallish fresh okra, trimmed at the top and bottom and cut into $\frac{1}{3}$-inch pieces

1 pound Swiss chard, chopped, stems and all

1 teaspoon ground cumin

$\frac{1}{4}$ teaspoon cayenne pepper

$4\frac{1}{2}$ cups chicken stock

l cup coconut milk from a well-shaken can

Salt, as needed

Pour the oil into a large pan and set over medium-high heat. When hot, put in the onions, carrots, beans, and okra. Sauté for 5 minutes. Add the chard, cumin, and cayenne. Sauté another 2–3 minutes. Now add half of the stock and bring to a boil. Cover, turn the heat to low, and simmer gently for about 25 minutes.

Put the soup in a blender and blend in as many batches as is necessary. Return the soup to the large pan. Add the remaining stock to thin the soup out, as well as the coconut milk. Stir to mix and taste for salt, adding as much as you need. Heat before serving.

Red Pepper Soup with Ginger and Fennel

This has always been a favorite soup of mine. I made it very recently with the last of the bell peppers on my plants. The leaves had shriveled already, but the peppers were still hanging on. It was such a cold, damp day that I decided to add some warming ginger to the soup for added comfort.

SERVES 6

2 pounds sweet red bell peppers
4 tablespoons olive or canola oil
1 medium onion, chopped
1 medium potato (about 4 ounces), peeled and chopped
One 1-inch piece fresh ginger, peeled and chopped
½ teaspoon whole fennel seeds

¼ teaspoon ground turmeric
1 teaspoon ground cumin seeds
¼ teaspoon cayenne pepper
5–5½ cups chicken stock or vegetable stock
1 teaspoon salt
5–6 tablespoons heavy cream

Chop the peppers coarsely after discarding all the seeds.

Pour the oil into a large, wide pan and set over medium-high heat. When hot, put in the peppers, onions, potatoes, ginger, fennel seeds, turmeric, cumin, and cayenne. Stir and fry until all the vegetables just start to brown. Add 2 cups of the stock and the salt. Stir and bring to a simmer. Cover, turn heat to low, and simmer gently for 25 minutes.

Ladle the soup in batches into a blender and blend until smooth. Pour the blended soup into a clean pot. Add the remaining stock, thinning the soup out as much as you like. Add the cream and mix it in. Adjust salt, as needed. Heat through before serving.

Red Lentil Curry Soup

Somewhere between the famous Mulligatawny Soup of the mixed-race Anglo-Indians and the soupy lentil-tomato-pasta dish, *dal dholki,* of the vegetarians of the western state of Gujarat, lies this soup. It is made with red lentils and tomatoes and may be served with a dollop of plain white rice or with some cooked pasta (pappardelle, noodles, macaroni) added to the soup just before it is heated for serving. This soup, plus a salad, makes for a perfect lunch or supper.

There are three simple steps to follow here. First you boil up the lentils. As they cook, you sauté the seasonings. Then you combine the two and blend them.

SERVES 4–6

FOR BOILING THE LENTILS

1 cup (7 ounces) red lentils (called *masoor dal* in Indian shops), well washed and drained

4 cups chicken stock or water (you will need a little more later for thinning out)

¼ teaspoon ground turmeric

1 medium carrot, peeled and chopped

A handful of washed cilantro (just rip some off the top of the bunch)

FOR SAUTÉING THE SEASONINGS

2 tablespoons olive or canola oil

6 tablespoons chopped onions

1 teaspoon finely grated peeled fresh ginger

1 teaspoon ground cumin

1 teaspoon ground coriander

1 teaspoon curry powder

⅛ teaspoon cayenne pepper

1½ cups (about 7 ounces) chopped fresh tomatoes

FOR FINISHING OFF THE SOUP

Salt

¾ cup chicken stock or water

Put the lentils and stock in a pan and bring to a boil. Skim off the white froth and add the turmeric, carrots, and cilantro. Stir, cover partially, and turn heat to low. Cook for 45 minutes.

While lentils are cooking, pour the oil into a frying pan and set on medium heat. When hot, put in the onions. Stir and fry until the pieces turn brown at the edges. Take pan off the heat and add the ginger, cumin, coriander, curry powder, and cayenne. Return the pan to the heat and stir for a minute. Add the tomatoes and ½ cup water. Cook, stirring now and then on medium heat, until the tomatoes are soft. Turn off heat.

When the lentils have cooked for 45 minutes, empty the contents of the frying pan into the lentil pan, stir, cover, and cook on low heat for 10 minutes, adding salt to taste. Blend the soup, adding another ¾ cup stock or water to swish out the remains sticking to the blender. Reheat the soup, stirring as you do so.

Spinach and Ginger Soup
Perfumed with Cloves

Here is a soup that is perfect for cold winter days, the ginger in it providing lasting warmth. The ginger also helps if you have a cold and acts as a stabilizer for those who suffer from travel sickness. Apart from all its health-giving properties (which Indians always have in the back of their heads), this is a delicious soup that can be served at any meal.

SERVES 4–6

4 cups chicken stock

10 ounces spinach, well washed and coarsely chopped

1 medium carrot, peeled and cut crossways into thick slices

1 medium (4 ounces) onion, coarsely chopped

1 large potato (8–9 ounces), peeled and coarsely chopped

½–1 fresh hot green chili, chopped (if using a jalapeño, use ¼)

One 1-inch piece fresh ginger, peeled and very finely chopped

2 whole cloves

10 black peppercorns

Salt

½ cup heavy cream, plus a little more for dribbling

2 teaspoons lemon juice

Pour the stock into a good-sized pan, and stir in the spinach, carrots, onions, potatoes, green chili, ginger, cloves, and peppercorns. Bring to a boil. Cover, turn heat to low, and simmer 20 minutes or until potatoes are tender.

Blend the soup in batches until smooth. Pour back into the pan through a coarse strainer, adding ¾ teaspoon salt (more if the stock was unsalted), the ½ cup cream, and the lemon juice. Mix and bring to a boil over medium heat, stirring and tasting for balance of seasonings. Dribble a little bit of cream on top of every serving, if desired.

Tomato-Lentil Soup

I make this a lot when tomatoes are in season. It makes for a simple, nutritious lunch or first course.

SERVES 4

1¾ pounds tomatoes, chopped
½ cup red lentils
2 cups chicken stock or water
1 tablespoon whole coriander seeds
1 teaspoon whole cumin seeds
¼ teaspoon ground turmeric
¼ teaspoon cayenne pepper, or to taste

½ medium onion, chopped
One 1-inch piece fresh ginger, peeled and chopped
A handful of cilantro
10–15 fresh curry leaves, if available, or 6 fresh basil leaves, torn up
1 teaspoon salt

Put all the ingredients except the salt into a pan and bring to a simmer. Cover partially, leaving the lid slightly ajar, turn the heat to low, and simmer very gently for an hour. Add the salt and mix in. Strain the soup through a coarse strainer, pushing down with the back of a wooden spoon. Reheat before serving, stirring as you go.

Gujarati-Style Tomato Soup

Gujaratis in western India do not actually drink soups as such. They do have many soupy dishes, which are meant to be eaten with flatbreads, rice, or spongy, savory, steamed cakes known as *dhoklas.* Here is one such dish. It makes for a gorgeous soup. I serve it with a little dollop of cream and a light sprinkling of ground roasted cumin (page 284), though these are not at all essential.

In the summer months, I make my own tomato puree and use that to make the soup. Store-bought puree is perfectly good too. In Gujarat a similar dish is served with homemade noodles in it. It is known as *dal dhokli.* I sometimes throw small quantities of cooked pasta bow ties or even macaroni into the soup.

SERVES 4

3 tablespoons olive or canola oil

$\frac{1}{8}$ teaspoon ground asafetida (optional)

$\frac{1}{2}$ teaspoon whole brown mustard seeds

$\frac{1}{2}$ teaspoon whole cumin seeds

2 tablespoons chickpea flour

4 cups chicken stock, vegetable stock, or water

2 cups tomato puree

About 20 fresh curry leaves or 6 basil leaves

$\frac{1}{4}$ teaspoon ground turmeric

$\frac{1}{8}$–$\frac{1}{4}$ teaspoon cayenne pepper

1 teaspoon salt, or a bit more, to taste

$1\frac{1}{2}$ teaspoons sugar, or to taste

Pour the oil into a large pan and set over medium-high heat. When hot, put in the asafetida, mustard, and cumin seeds. As soon as the mustard seeds begin to pop, a matter of seconds, add the chickpea flour. Turn the heat to medium low. Stir a few times with a whisk, until the chickpea flour turns a shade darker. Slowly add the stock, stirring with a whisk as you go. When well mixed and thick, add the tomato puree, mixing as you go, then the curry leaves, turmeric, cayenne, salt, and sugar. Bring to a boil. Turn heat to low and simmer 25 minutes. Turn off the heat and leave the soup in the pan as long as possible, allowing the spices to release more of their flavors. Push through a strainer and reheat before serving.

TOMATO PUREE

I grow my own tomatoes, and when they ripen they all seem to ripen at once. I cannot eat them all in their fresh form—though I do try—so I have to preserve them in some way. For those who do not grow their own tomatoes, summer farmstands carry tons of ripe tomatoes at good prices. Buy them and preserve them.

For me, the most useful way is to make a puree, which I freeze in small quantities in half-cup canning jars. It defrosts quickly, and I can use it to flavor everything from fish to vegetables.

HOW TO MAKE YOUR OWN TOMATO PUREE

Wash the tomatoes and let them dry. Chop them coarsely after removing the sepals and stems, and put them into a pan that can hold them easily. Crush the tomato pieces first with your hands to release their juices, then turn the heat on medium low and let the tomatoes come to a simmer slowly. The low heat allows more juices to ooze out slowly. Add just a tiny bit of salt, as this helps release the juices. Once the tomatoes are bubbling, turn the heat up to medium and let them simmer vigorously until you have a thick sauce, stirring now and then so it does not catch on the bottom of the pan. Let the tomatoes cool off and push them through a coarse strainer or put them in a blender. Pour the puree into $\frac{1}{2}$-cup canning jars, cover, and freeze.

Fish and Seafood

ndians, Pakistanis, Bangladeshis, and Sri Lankans eat much more fish than you may surmise from dining at their restaurants abroad. The countries of South Asia have long coastlines dotted with fish-market towns selling everything from the smallest of cockles to the largest marlins, kingfish, and swordfish—all fresh, hauled in the same day.

From the sea there are red snappers and black groupers to be had, as well as silver pomfrets that might well be steamed in banana leaves or cooked in creamy coconut sauces. There are sardines to put into fiery Kerala curries and kingfish to be pan-fried with turmeric and chilies. From the estuaries where rivers meet the sea, there are shrimp and crabs to be collected and cooked with mustard seeds or coconut milk. The shadlike hilsa flows upstream in some rivers and is wonderful steamed in a mustard sauce or smoked. Mountain streams are well stocked with trout, which anglers deep-fry on site and eat with a salt and Kashmiri chili powder dip. The rice paddies are filled with catfish and eels and the mighty rivers of the Gangetic Plain with delicate-fleshed Indian fish, *singhara* and *rahu.* All are caught and eaten.

In many parts of India, it is a tradition to rub cut pieces of fish with a little salt and turmeric before cooking. The salt firms up the fish so it does not disintegrate in the pan, and turmeric is an antiseptic. Indians have done this for thousands of years. In Bengal, in eastern India, and in Bangladesh, a thin sauce made with crushed mustard seeds, chili powder, and turmeric is much loved, while in Kerala small fish such as sardines and whitebait are washed in a lime-water solution,

41

dipped in rice flour, and deep-fried. In Pakistan fish rubbed with ajowan seeds (of the thyme family) are roasted briefly in a fiercely hot *tandoor* oven, and in Sri Lanka you might be served fish perfumed with fennel seeds and poached in coconut milk.

You will find some of these recipes in this chapter, designed for fish that is available in Western markets.

CLOCKWISE FROM TOP: *Chili Powder, Turmeric, and Salt*

Tandoori-Style Striped Bass Fillet

One of the characteristics of tandoori fish in the Punjab, where tandoori—or clay-oven-baked—meat and fish dishes originated, is that they are flavored with ajowan seeds. These tiny seeds look rather like small celery seeds, except that their main aroma comes from thymol, which you find in thyme as well. Instead of using ajowan (ajwain in India), I have simplified matters by using the more easily available thyme instead.

Serving suggestions: For a very light meal, you can serve this fish with a salad. You could also make a more substantial meal by offering some rice and either Spinach with Garlic and Cumin or Swiss Chard with Ginger and Garlic.

SERVES 2–3

1 pound striped bass fillet—
    a 1½-inch-thick center cut is ideal
Salt
¼–½ teaspoon cayenne pepper
⅛ teaspoon ground turmeric
Freshly ground black pepper
2 tablespoons oil

2 tablespoons melted *ghee* or melted
    butter
1 tablespoon lemon juice
½ teaspoon ground cumin
8–10 sprigs of fresh thyme, or
    1 teaspoon dried thyme

Dust the top of the fillet with ¼ teaspoon salt, the cayenne, the turmeric, and lots of black pepper. Pat the spices in. Cover and refrigerate from 1 to 6 hours.

Preheat the oven to 500°F.

Lay the fish out on a baking tray, skin side down. Combine the oil, melted *ghee* or butter, lemon juice, cumin, and ¼ teaspoon salt in a small bowl and mix well. Spread this evenly over the top of the fish. Scatter the thyme sprigs over the top as well and place in the top third of the oven. Bake, brushing frequently with the juices, until the fish turns opaque all over, 25 minutes or less, depending upon the thickness of the fillet.

Pakistani Tandoori-Style Fish

We sat on cushions at an open-air, rooftop restaurant in Peshawar, Pakistan. As it was winter, we had been offered quilts to cover our legs and small individual braziers to keep at our sides. The glow of *tandoor* clay ovens just a few paces away offered added consolation. It was from there that this fish dish emerged. It was a river fish caught nearby, cooked whole in the *tandoor* until its outside was browned and the inside was flaky and soft. It was the spices that gave the fish its kick. I asked the chef for the recipe, and here it is. I have had to make a few changes. Instead of the river fish I have used Spanish mackerel (you could also use filleted trout); instead of quick-roasting in a *tandoor* I pan-fry; instead of ajowan seeds, I have used dried thyme (both contain thymol); and instead of sour oranges I have used a mixture of lemon and sugar. It still tastes marvelous. In Peshawar, this was served with a simple Vinegar-Chili-Onion Dipping Sauce. That recipe is on page 242. You could serve this Western style with boiled parsley potatoes and some green beans, or with Carrots with Cilantro and Potatoes with Cumin and Mustard Seeds.

SERVES 2–3

2 teaspoons very finely grated peeled fresh ginger

1 teaspoon finely crushed garlic

1 teaspoon ground cumin

1 teaspoon dried thyme (if ajowan seeds are available, use ¼ teaspoon)

¼ teaspoon freshly ground black pepper

¼–½ teaspoon cayenne pepper

1 teaspoon nice red paprika

½ teaspoon *garam masala,* preferably homemade (see page 285)

¼ teaspoon ground turmeric

1 tablespoon lemon juice

¼ teaspoon sugar

¾ teaspoon salt

1–1¼-pound fillet of Spanish mackerel or mackerel, cut crossways into 3-inch pieces

2 tablespoons olive or canola oil

Mix together in a small bowl the ginger, garlic, cumin, thyme, black pepper, cayenne, paprika, *garam masala,* turmeric, lemon juice, sugar, and salt. Put this paste on both sides of the fish pieces—it will adhere better to the fleshy side—and set aside for 30 minutes.

Put 1 tablespoon of the oil in a nonstick frying pan and set on medium-high heat. When hot, put in half of the fish pieces, flesh side down, and cook about 2 minutes or until nicely browned. Turn over and brown the skin side for another 2 minutes. Remove to a dish and leave in warm place. Quickly wipe the pan out with a paper towel, put in the remaining 1 tablespoon oil, and cook the rest of the fish the same way.

Grilled Masala Salmon

In India we frequently use a paste of ground mustard seeds. I have simplified matters here and used already-prepared Dijon mustard instead.

You could serve this with Basmati Rice with Lentils and South Indian–Style Green Beans.

SERVES 2

⅛ teaspoon salt
¼ teaspoon ground cumin
⅛ teaspoon ground coriander
⅛ teaspoon ground turmeric
¼ teaspoon cayenne pepper
¾-pound skinned salmon fillet

2 tablespoons Dijon mustard
  (the plain kind)
1 tablespoon olive or canola oil
2 teaspoons lemon juice
2 tablespoons finely chopped cilantro

Rub the salt, cumin, coriander, turmeric, and cayenne all over the fish. Cover and refrigerate 1–4 hours.

Heat the broiler.

Mix the mustard, oil, and lemon juice in a small bowl. Add the cilantro. Rub this all over the fish and place under the broiler, about 5 inches from the source of heat. When the top has browned lightly, about 4 minutes, turn the oven to "bake," setting the temperature at 350°F. Bake about 10 minutes or until the fish is cooked through.

Delicious Pan-Grilled Halibut
(or Swordfish, or Salmon)

If you are looking for a superbly elegant, gentle dish, look no further. In a long line of meats and seafood grilled after they have been marinated very simply in a paste of fresh ginger, garlic, and chilies, this dish is a great family favorite. Have the fishmonger remove the halibut skin.

I like to serve this with Karhai Broccoli and a potato or rice dish.

SERVES 4

One 1¼-pound section of skinned
    halibut fillet, ¾–1 inch thick
    (salmon or swordfish may be used
    instead)
½ teaspoon salt
¼ teaspoon ground turmeric
2 teaspoons finely grated peeled fresh
    ginger

2 cloves garlic, mashed in a garlic press
1 tablespoon lemon juice
¼ teaspoon cayenne pepper, or more,
    if you prefer
1 tablespoon rice flour (use white flour
    as a substitute)
4 tablespoons olive or canola oil

Cut the halibut into 4 segments. Rub the salt and turmeric all over and set aside for 20 minutes.

Meanwhile, combine the ginger, garlic, lemon juice, and cayenne in a small bowl. Mix. After the fish has sat in the salt mixture for 20 minutes, rub the ginger mixture on all sides, patting it in, then cover and refrigerate 20–30 minutes.

Preheat oven to 350°F.

Dust the top and bottom of the marinade-covered fish pieces with the rice flour and pat it in.

Line a small baking tray with foil. Set aside.

Put the oil on a nonstick frying pan and set over medium-high heat. When hot, put in the fish pieces in a single layer, with one of the rice flour–covered sides down. Let that side brown, about a minute, and then turn to brown the opposite side. Once that has happened, remove fish pieces carefully to the baking tray and place in the oven for 10 minutes or until just cooked through.

Masala Fish Steaks

You can use almost any fish steaks here—salmon, kingfish, cod, haddock, swordfish, salmon, trout, pomfret, pompano, or tilefish—depending on the part of the world you live in.

Instead of having to look for ajowan seeds (use ¼ teaspoon, if you can get them), you can use dried thyme, which has the same flavor.

When using the blender here, make sure you put the chopped red pepper in first, as that will provide the liquid needed to make a paste. If your blender remains stubborn, add a tablespoon or two of water.

You could serve this with Zucchini and Yellow Summer Squash with Cumin, and Bulgar Pilaf with Peas and Tomato.

SERVES 2–4

1 pound fish steaks (see above)
Salt
½ large red bell pepper (half of a 6-ounce pepper), seeds removed, chopped
4 cloves garlic, chopped

One 1-inch piece fresh ginger, peeled and chopped
¼ teaspoon dried thyme
1 small onion, chopped
½ teaspoon cayenne pepper
Vegetable oil for shallow frying
Lime or lemon juice

Sprinkle the fish with ¼ teaspoon salt on both sides and set aside, in the refrigerator if necessary.

Put the red peppers, garlic, ginger, thyme, ¾ teaspoon salt, onions, and cayenne into a blender in that order and make a paste.

Put the oil in a frying pan (you should have ¼ inch of oil) and set on medium-high heat. When hot, put in the fish steaks and fry until light brown on both sides. Transfer with a slotted spoon to a plate. Remove all but 5 table-spoons of the oil, and put back on medium-high heat. When hot, add the paste from the blender. Stir and fry for about 3 minutes or until the paste seems to dry out. Turn heat down and fry another 2 minutes. Put the fish back in the pan, add 2 tablespoons water, and cook the fish through on very low heat, spooning the sauce over the fish. Squeeze lime juice over the top.

Fish Fillets with Spicy Green Undercoat

Here I use boneless fish fillets with skin—porgies, red snapper, mackerel, bluefish, gray mullet, redfish, trout, or anything else of modest size. If the fillets are too long, I cut them into convenient 3–4-inch lengths so I can turn them easily in a frying pan.

The spicy undercoat is made simply in a food processor or chopper, though you could chop finely by hand if you prefer.

If you want to keep the meal simple, serve this fish with Potato Chaat and Spinach with Garlic and Cumin or a salad.

SERVES 3–4

FOR THE SPICY GREEN UNDERCOATING

5 good-sized cherry tomatoes, halved
1 tablespoon lemon juice
1 well-packed cup cilantro (use only the tops, not the stems)
2 bird's-eye chilies (or half of a jalapeño), chopped
3 cloves garlic
One $1\frac{1}{2}$-inch piece fresh ginger, peeled and chopped
$\frac{1}{2}$ teaspoon salt

YOU ALSO NEED

1–$1\frac{1}{4}$-pound fish fillets with skin (see above for suggestions)
1 cup plain white flour
Olive or canola oil for frying, enough to have $\frac{1}{4}$ inch in a large frying pan

Combine all the ingredients for the spicy green coating in a food processor or chopper. Chop until you have a fine, granular sauce. Empty into a large glass or stainless-steel bowl. Add the fillets and mix well. Set aside 20–30 minutes, not much longer.

Take the fish fillets out of the marinade, shaking out the liquid, and lay them in a plate in a single layer. With a slotted spoon, extract the solids from the marinade bowl and pat them all over both sides of the fillets.

Spread the flour out on a large plate. Now dip the fillets carefully, one at a time, in the flour on both sides and lay them side by side in a fresh plate.

Set a large frying pan or sauté pan with $\frac{1}{4}$-inch oil over medium-high heat. When hot, slip the fillets into the oil and fry 3–4 minutes per side until reddish brown. Drain on paper towels and serve hot.

Fish and Peas in a Fennel-Fenugreek Sauce

I used to make this dish with fillets of halibut until the cost, at least in New York, made me look at other fish. Now I use cod or hake. They both flake a bit more but still manage to hold their shape. Salting them ahead of time helps hold them together.

I like to use fresh tomatoes even if they are out of season, as they are gentler in flavor. I grate the tomatoes on the coarsest part of a four-sided grater (see method on page 289), which removes the skin but keeps the seeds. Four medium tomatoes will yield roughly 1¾ cups of fresh puree, about what you need here.

Light and lovely, this dish is best served with rice. I like to add a *dal* and perhaps a green, leafy vegetable.

SERVES 2–3

1 pound fillet of cod, hake,
    or halibut, ½–¾ inch thick
Salt
Freshly ground black pepper
Cayenne pepper
⅛ teaspoon ground turmeric
3 tablespoons mustard, olive, or
    canola oil
⅛ teaspoon ground asafetida
¼ teaspoon whole mustard seeds

½ teaspoon whole cumin seeds
¼ teaspoon whole fennel seeds
⅛ teaspoon whole fenugreek seeds
3 tablespoons plain yogurt, preferably
    the acidophilus variety sold at
    health-food stores, or Greek yogurt
4 medium tomatoes, coarsely grated
1 cup fresh or frozen and defrosted
    peas

Sprinkle the fish on both sides with ¼ teaspoon salt, freshly ground black pepper, ¼ teaspoon cayenne, and the ground turmeric. Set aside 30 minutes or longer, refrigerating if necessary.

Put the oil in a frying pan and set on medium-high heat. When hot, put in the asafetida and then the mustard, cumin, fennel, and fenugreek seeds. As soon as the mustard seeds start to pop, a matter of seconds, put in the yogurt. Stir the yogurt on medium-high heat until it almost disappears. Add the tomatoes, ¾ teaspoon salt, ¼ teaspoon cayenne, and some black pepper. Stir and cook for 5 minutes or until tomatoes thicken slightly. Add the peas, stir, and continue to cook another minute on medium heat. Lay the fish down in this sauce. If there is a thinnish tail end, tuck it under. Spoon the sauce over the fish and bring to a simmer. Cover, leaving the lid slightly ajar, and poach fish on medium-low heat, spooning the sauce over the fish now and then, until it is just cooked through, about 7–10 minutes. If the pan seems to dry out, add a few tablespoons of water.

Salmon in a Bengali Mustard Sauce

Eat this with plain rice and make the sauce as hot as you like. In Bengal, the mustard seeds are ground at home, but to make matters simpler I have used commercial ground mustard, also sold as mustard powder. You may also use halibut instead of the salmon.

This very traditional dish is best served with Plain Basmati Rice, along with My Everyday Moong Dal, if you like, and a green vegetable.

SERVES 2–3

TO RUB ON THE FISH
¾ pound skinless salmon fillet
¼ teaspoon salt
¼ teaspoon ground turmeric
¼ teaspoon cayenne pepper

YOU ALSO NEED
1 tablespoon ground mustard
¼–½ teaspoon cayenne pepper
¼ teaspoon ground turmeric
¼ teaspoon salt
2 tablespoons mustard oil (use extra virgin olive oil as a substitute)
¼ teaspoon whole brown mustard seeds
¼ teaspoon whole cumin seeds
¼ teaspoon whole fennel seeds
2 fresh hot green and/or red chilies (bird's-eye is best), slit slightly

Cut the fish into pieces that are about 2" × 1" and rub them evenly with the salt, turmeric, and cayenne. Cover and set aside in the refrigerator for 30 minutes–10 hours.

Put the mustard powder, cayenne, turmeric, and salt in a small bowl. Add 1 tablespoon water and mix thoroughly. Add another 7 tablespoons water and mix. Set aside.

Pour the oil into a medium frying pan and set over medium-high heat. When hot, put in the mustard seeds. As soon as they start to pop, a matter of seconds, add the cumin and fennel seeds. Stir once and quickly pour in the mustard paste. Add the green chilies, stir, and bring to a gentle simmer. Place the fish pieces in the sauce in a single layer. Simmer gently for about 5 minutes, or until the fish is just cooked through, spooning the sauce over the fish all the time.

OVERLEAF: *Salmon in Bengali Mustard Sauce with Basmati Rice*

Salmon in a Tomato-Cream Sauce

I first had this sauce, or one similar to it, in the late 1940s. India had just been partitioned, and a refugee family fleeing from what was to become Pakistan had just opened a small, simple restaurant in the center of Delhi called Moti Mahal. It basically served foods baked in the clay oven called a *tandoor*. There was one sauced dish, however, Chicken Makhani. A *tandoor*-roasted chicken was cut up with a cleaver and then heated up in this tomatoey, buttery, creamy sauce. I have always loved the sauce. Over the years, I have played around with it, using it with shrimp, and now with salmon. Serve with Swiss Chard with Ginger and Garlic and Rice Pilaf with Almonds and Raisins.

SERVES 4

TO RUB ON THE FISH

$1\frac{1}{2}$ pounds skinned salmon fillet from the center of the fish (where it is thickest), first cut lengthways down the center and then crossways to make 8 pieces

$\frac{1}{4}$ teaspoon salt

Freshly ground black pepper

$\frac{1}{8}$ teaspoon ground turmeric

$\frac{1}{8}$ teaspoon cayenne pepper

FOR THE SAUCE

1 cup tomato puree

1 cup heavy cream

1 teaspoon salt

1 teaspoon sugar

1 teaspoon *garam masala*

1 teaspoon ground cumin

1 tablespoon lemon juice

$\frac{1}{8}$ teaspoon cayenne pepper

2 tablespoons chopped cilantro

TO COOK THE FISH

1 tablespoon olive or canola oil

$\frac{1}{2}$ teaspoon whole cumin seeds

Season the salmon pieces by sprinkling the salt, pepper, turmeric, and cayenne on all sides and rubbing them in. Put the salmon in a plastic bag and refrigerate for 1 hour or longer.

Combine all the ingredients for the sauce and mix well. Refrigerate if needed.

To cook the fish, put the oil in a frying pan and set on medium heat. When hot, put in the cumin seeds. When the seeds have sizzled for 10 seconds, pour in the sauce. Stir and bring to a simmer. Place all the fish pieces in the sauce in a single layer and cook, spooning the sauce over the fish. After a minute, turn the fish pieces over and lower the heat to medium low. Continue to cook, spooning the sauce over the top, for 3–4 minutes or until the fish has cooked through.

Bangladeshi Fish Curry

In Bangladesh, the basic diet is fish and rice. It is not fish from the Bay of Bengal, the sea that rules their shores, that the people thrive on. In fact, they hardly touch that. What they love is the sweet-water fish that comes from their estuaries, rivers, lakes, and ponds.

Since local Bangladeshi fish are unavailable to most of us, I have adapted this recipe to fillet of flounder. One of the common local seasonings is an aromatic lime leaf very similar to the kaffir lime leaf of Thailand. If you cannot get that, use fresh curry leaves, or, failing that, fresh basil leaves.

Serve with plain rice, a *dal,* and a vegetable or salad.

SERVES 4

Salt

1–1¼-pound fillet of flounder (2 large fillets are ideal)

1½ teaspoons crushed garlic (use a garlic press)

1½ teaspoons very finely grated peeled fresh ginger (use a fine microplane)

¼ teaspoon ground turmeric

½ teaspoon cayenne pepper

1 teaspoon nice red paprika

3 tablespoons olive or mustard oil

⅓ cup finely sliced shallots

3 fresh torn kaffir lime leaves or 10 lightly crushed curry leaves or 5 basil leaves, torn up

Sprinkle ¼ teaspoon salt on both sides of the flounder fillets. Cut each fillet this way: First cut a 3-inch portion off the tail end. Now cut the remaining fillet in half lengthways and then cut crossways into 3-inch segments. Set all the pieces aside as you prepare the sauce.

Combine the garlic, ginger, turmeric, cayenne, paprika, ¼ teaspoon salt, and 3 tablespoons water in a bowl. Mix well to make a paste.

Pour the oil into a very large frying pan or sauté pan (a 12-inch diameter is ideal) and set on medium heat. When hot, put in the shallots. Stir and fry until they are lightly browned. Now put in the spice paste. Stir and fry for a minute. Add 1 cup water and the kaffir lime leaves. Stir and bring to a simmer. Simmer on low heat for 1 minute. Turn off the heat.

Just before serving, bring the sauce to a simmer over low heat. Lay the fish pieces in the sauce in a single layer. Cook 1 minute and turn the fish pieces over carefully. Cook another 2–3 minutes, spooning the sauce over the top, until the fish is just done.

Sri Lankan Fish Curry

In Sri Lanka, an island nation, fish is a staple. It is used in salads, as stuffing for savory pastries, as a flavoring in relishes, as a snack food with drinks, and, of course, in hundreds of curries. This particular curry was served to me for breakfast on a sunny patio at Castlereigh, a tea planter's home turned boutique hotel, along with fresh rice noodles and good, hot tea. On that cool morning in the mountains nothing could have tasted finer.

Almost any fish may be used here, as long as it is firm and holds its shape—swordfish, salmon, pompano, sole, haddock, kingfish, and mackerel. I have used swordfish.

Serve with Plain Jasmine Rice and Gujarati-Style Okra.

SERVES 2–3

1 pound boneless swordfish, ¾–1-inch thick, skin removed
Salt
3 tablespoons olive or canola oil
¼ teaspoon whole brown mustard seeds
¼ teaspoon whole fennel seeds
⅓ cup finely chopped red onions

1 clove garlic, chopped
15–20 fresh curry leaves or 10 fresh basil leaves, torn up
1 medium tomato, chopped
⅛ teaspoon ground turmeric
¼–½ teaspoon cayenne pepper
½ cup coconut milk from a well-shaken can

Cut the swordfish crossways into as many pieces as there are diners. Sprinkle each piece lightly with ¼ teaspoon salt on both sides.

Put the oil in a frying pan and set over medium-high heat. When hot, put in the mustard seeds. As soon as the mustard seeds begin to pop, a matter of seconds, put in the fennel seeds and then the onions. Stir and fry on medium heat until the onions soften a bit, about 2–3 minutes. Add the garlic and curry leaves. Stir another minute. Now add the tomatoes, turmeric, and cayenne. Stir a minute. Add ½ cup water and ½ teaspoon salt. Stir and bring to a simmer. Cover, turn heat to low, and cook gently for 10 minutes. Put the fish into this sauce and cook on medium-low heat for 3–4 minutes or until one side of the fish turns opaque. Turn the fish pieces over. Add the coconut milk, stir the sauce gently, and bring to a simmer again on medium heat, spooning the sauce over the fish. When the fish turns opaque all the way through, it is done.

Kerala-Style Fish Curry

I used a thick fillet of wild sea bass with skin here, cut into 3-inch segments. Use whatever fish looks good and fresh—haddock, halibut, salmon (steaks or thick fillet pieces), kingfish steaks, or even mackerel pieces. This is a creamy curry best eaten with rice. In Kerala it looks red from all the hot chili powder in it, but I have softened the heat with some paprika, which helps with the color.

Serve with Plain Jasmine Rice and South Indian–Style Green Beans.

SERVES 2–4

1–1¼ pounds wild sea bass fillet with skin, ½–¾-inch thick, cut crossways into 3-inch segments

Salt

2 tablespoons olive or canola oil

⅔ cup very finely slivered shallots

1 teaspoon finely grated peeled fresh ginger

1 large clove garlic, crushed in a garlic press

½ teaspoon ground turmeric

½ teaspoon cayenne pepper, or to taste

1 tablespoon nice red paprika

Lots of freshly ground black pepper

1 tablespoon lemon juice

½ cup coconut milk from a well-shaken can

Spread the fish pieces out and sprinkle ½ teaspoon salt on both sides. Set aside as you prepare the sauce.

Pour the oil into a frying pan and set over medium-high heat. When hot, put in the shallots. Stir and fry until the pieces just start to turn brown at the edges. Add the ginger and garlic. Stir for a minute. Now add 1 cup water, the turmeric, cayenne, paprika, black pepper, lemon juice, and ½ teaspoon salt. Bring to a simmer. Turn heat to low and simmer gently for 5 minutes, stirring now and then. Add the coconut milk and mix it in. Bring the sauce back to a simmer. Put the fish pieces in the pan in a single layer and cook on medium-low heat, spooning the sauce over the fish pieces until they are poached, 5–10 minutes.

Fish in a Fennel-Flavored Curry Sauce

Some version of this fish curry is eaten all along India's long coastline. I like to make it with fillets (with skin) of Spanish mackerel, but any mackerel or kingfish, indeed, any fish that does not flake too easily, will do. This cooks quickly and easily.

This dish is perfect with rice. Add a green vegetable and a salad as well.

SERVES 2–3

Salt

¾-pound fillet of Spanish mackerel, or see above for other fish, cut crossways into 3-inch segments

2 teaspoons finely grated peeled fresh ginger

1 teaspoon finely crushed garlic (just put it through a press)

¼–½ teaspoon cayenne pepper, or more, if desired

2 teaspoons nice red paprika

Freshly ground black pepper

¼ teaspoon ground turmeric

1 tablespoon lemon juice

2 tablespoons olive or canola oil

¼ teaspoon whole fennel seeds

3 tablespoons finely chopped shallots or red onions

¼ cup coconut milk from a well-shaken can or heavy cream

Rub about ⅛ teaspoon salt on both sides of the fish and set aside while you prepare all the remaining ingredients.

Combine the ginger, garlic, cayenne, paprika, black pepper, turmeric, lemon juice, and ½ teaspoon salt in a small bowl. Mix.

Put the oil in a frying pan—preferably nonstick—and set over medium-high heat. When hot, put in the fennel seeds and, a few seconds later, the shallots. Lower heat to medium. Stir and sauté the shallots until they soften slightly. Now add the seasonings from the bowl. Stir for a minute. Add 1 cup water, stir, and bring to a simmer. Turn heat to low and simmer gently, uncovered, for 7–8 minutes. Add the coconut milk or cream. Stir and bring to a simmer again. Slip in the fish pieces so they lie in the sauce, skin side down, in a single layer. Keep spooning the sauce over the fish pieces and cook gently 6–7 minutes or until the fish turns opaque.

Spicy Shrimp Stir-Fry (Bhuni Jhinga)

Here is a very quick way to stir-fry shrimp so they are encrusted with spices. They are hot, sour, and utterly delicious. The dish may be served as a first course, as a light lunch with a salad, or as part of a larger Indian meal.

Sri Lankan Rice with Cilantro and Lemon Grass goes well with this, as well as the Mushroom and Pea Curry.

SERVES 4

1 pound raw medium shrimp, peeled and deveined (or 12 ounces peeled and deveined medium shrimp)

¼ teaspoon ground turmeric

⅛–¼ teaspoon cayenne pepper, or to taste

1 teaspoon ground coriander

½ teaspoon ground cumin

¼ teaspoon salt

2 tablespoons olive, canola, or peanut oil

¼ teaspoon whole brown or yellow mustard seeds

¼ teaspoon whole cumin seeds

1 good-sized clove garlic, chopped

1½ teaspoons lemon juice

Wash the shrimp well. Leave in a strainer for a while and then pat dry. Put in a bowl with the turmeric, cayenne, coriander, cumin, and salt. Mix well.

Pour the oil into a frying pan and set over medium-high heat. When hot, put in the mustard and cumin seeds. As soon as the mustard seeds begin to pop, a matter of seconds, put in the garlic and stir once or twice. Quickly add the shrimp and stir once or twice. Turn the heat down immediately to medium low and let the shrimp cook gently, stirring as you do so, until they just turn opaque all through, a matter of 2 or 3 minutes. Add the lemon juice and toss to mix. Serve immediately.

Goan Shrimp Curry

Goa, on India's west coast, is tropical, by the sea, and a haven for tourists from Israel, Germany, the United Kingdom, and, indeed, the entire affluent world, which cannot get enough of its easy ways, its sun and sand. Some of the best food in Goa is not in its expensive resorts but in thatched shacks right on the sea. The fish is always fresh, and usually nothing can beat the fiery shrimp (called prawns here) curry, served with a mound of short-grained local rice.

Serve with Plain Jasmine Rice and a green or salad of your choice.

SERVES 4

2 tablespoons olive or canola oil

2 finely chopped medium shallots

¼ teaspoon or more cayenne pepper, as preferred

2 teaspoons bright red paprika

½ teaspoon freshly ground black pepper

¼ teaspoon ground turmeric

1¼ cups coconut milk from a well-shaken can

1 pound large or medium shrimp, peeled and deveined (or 12 ounces peeled and deveined shrimp)

½ teaspoon salt

1–2 teaspoons lemon juice

Pour the oil into a frying pan or sauté pan and set over medium heat. When hot, put in the shallots. Stir and fry until they turn light brown. Take the pan off the heat and add the cayenne, paprika, black pepper, and turmeric. Stir once or twice and put the pan back on the heat. Add the coconut milk and bring to a simmer, stirring to mix. Turn heat to low. Put in the shrimp, salt, and lemon juice. Stir and cook on low heat until the shrimp just turn opaque.

Squid is now available all cleaned and ready to cook. All you have to do is cut it up as you desire. It is very simple to cook if you know its idiosyncrasies. Since it can get tough very easily, you have to either cook squid very fast, for 1–2 minutes on very high heat, or stew it slowly and gently for at least 45 minutes. The former results in a firm texture while the latter makes the squid pieces pliable and soft. The next two recipes give examples of both techniques.

Stir-Fried Squid with Mustard Seeds

Here is a quick stir-fry that you might serve with Plain Jasmine Rice and Corn with Aromatic Seasonings.

SERVES 3–4

1 pound cleaned squid
2 cloves garlic, crushed to a pulp
1 teaspoon salt
4 tablespoons well-chopped cilantro
$\frac{1}{4}$–$\frac{1}{2}$ teaspoon cayenne pepper
1 tablespoon chickpea flour
10–15 fresh curry leaves, or 6 fresh
    basil leaves

3 tablespoons olive or canola oil
$\frac{1}{2}$ teaspoon whole brown mustard
    seeds
2 dried hot red chilies
1 tablespoon lemon juice
Freshly ground black pepper

Cut the bodies of the squid crossways into $\frac{1}{4}$-inch-thick rings and separate the tentacles, cutting up those that seem very long. Wash well, drain in a colander, and then pat dry. Combine the squid, garlic, salt, cilantro, cayenne, chickpea flour, and curry leaves in a bowl. Mix well and set aside for 15 minutes.

Put the oil in a nonstick frying pan and set over medium-high heat. When hot, put in the mustard seeds. As soon as they start to pop, a matter of seconds, put in the red chilies. They will darken quickly. Now put in the squid and spice mixture from the bowl. Stir and fry on high heat for $1\frac{1}{2}$–2 minutes. Turn off the heat. Add the lemon juice and black pepper. Stir to mix.

Squid Curry

Make this curry as fiery hot as you like. That is how it is preferred in many parts of South India. This dish is generally served with plain rice or with the thin, fresh rice noodles known as *idiappam*. I have given a method of preparing dried rice sticks, sold in Thai and Vietnamese markets, on page 224 (see Thin Rice Noodles). They are the closest to the Indian noodles. I have also been known to serve this curry over thin spaghettini or angel-hair pasta.

SERVES 3–4

1 pound cleaned squid

2 tablespoons olive or canola oil

½ teaspoon whole brown mustard seeds

1 medium onion, cut into fine half rings

15 fresh curry leaves or 10 fresh basil leaves

1 teaspoon finely grated peeled fresh ginger

1 clove garlic, crushed

1 tablespoon curry powder (I use Bolst's Hot Curry Powder, but any will do)

2 tablespoons tomato paste

¾ teaspoon salt

1 tablespoon lemon juice

Cut the bodies of the squid crossways into ¼-inch-thick rings and separate the tentacles, cutting up those that seem very long. Wash well and leave to drain in a colander.

Pour the oil into a frying pan and set over medium-high heat. When hot, put in the mustard seeds. As soon as they start to pop, a matter of seconds, put in the onions and the curry leaves. Stir and fry until the onions just start to turn brown at the edges. Add the ginger, garlic, and curry powder. Stir for a minute. Add the tomato paste and stir a few times. Now add 2 cups water, the salt, lemon juice, and squid. Stir and bring to a simmer on gentle heat. Simmer the squid, covered, on low heat, stirring now and then, for about 45 minutes or until the squid is tender.

Mussels in a Creamy Coconut Sauce

Here is a dish much beloved by my husband and children. Medium-sized clams may be substituted for the mussels.

You may serve this as a first course, as the main course, or as a light lunch with a salad. Indians eat this curry with rice, but you may serve the mussels by themselves in individual bowls.

SERVES 2–4

2 pounds medium-sized mussels

2 tablespoons olive or canola oil

½ teaspoon whole brown mustard seeds

1 good-sized onion (about 6 ounces), finely chopped

1 teaspoon finely grated peeled fresh ginger

1 teaspoon crushed garlic

1¾ cups coconut milk, from a well-shaken can

2 teaspoons ground cumin seeds

¼ teaspoon cayenne pepper

¾ teaspoon salt

15 fresh curry leaves or 10 fresh basil leaves, crushed in the palm of your hand

4 tablespoons finely chopped cilantro

2 fresh hot green chilies (bird's-eye is ideal), partially slit

1 tablespoon lemon juice

Scrub the mussels well with a brush, discarding those that remain open even after they are tapped. Pull off any stringy beards.

Put the oil in a large pot and set over medium-high heat. When hot, put in the mustard seeds. As soon as the mustard seeds start to pop, a matter of seconds, put in the onions and turn the heat down to medium. Stir and cook 4–5 minutes or until the onions have softened. Add the ginger and garlic. Stir for a minute. Now add the coconut milk, 1 cup water, the cumin, cayenne, salt, curry leaves, cilantro, green chilies, and lemon juice. Stir and bring to a simmer. Simmer gently, uncovered, stirring now and then, for 5 minutes. (This much can be done ahead of time.) Add all the mussels and bring to a boil on medium-high heat. Cover and cook rapidly for 5 minutes or until all the mussels have opened (discard any that stay closed).

OVERLEAF: *Soft-Boiled Eggs with Seasoned Salt*

Eggs and Poultry

I love eggs. In every form. There is nothing finer than a soft-boiled egg perched in an egg cup, ready to be eaten with a mixture of salt, pepper, and a tiny bit of ground, roasted cumin seeds. Or poached eggs served over Potatoes with Cumin and Mustard Seeds. Then, there are Indian omelettes and scrambled eggs. Every household makes these its own way: some put in onions, others don't; some add tomatoes, others leave them out; there is a choice of using ginger or turmeric or cumin seeds or mustard seeds; certain flavorings seem to be constant—cilantro and green or red chilies.

Whenever my friend the late producer Ismail Merchant flew into town, he would call up and say, "Come over for dinner." The fact that his cupboard was completely bare and his refrigerator mostly empty from weeks abroad did not faze him one bit. He bought some eggs and made an egg curry, which he served with rice, his mother's mango pickle, and some salad. What more could one want? Egg curries generally require nothing more than hard-boiled eggs, a few spices, and something to provide a sauce, such as tomatoes or coconut milk.

Rather like real estate, the value of chicken goes up and down. And I do not mean its price, though that is connected. Chicken, which is native to the Indian subcontinent, was once a special treat, reserved for festive occasions. Such was the case when I was growing up in India. Chicken was expensive. Then came the era of massive chicken farms with the birds all cooped up one on top of another, fed all kinds of chemicals and medicines so they would grow plump fast and not die of diseases sweeping the coops. The price of chicken fell, and so did its status. Now better-quality, organic, and hormone-free and free-range chickens are being sold (at higher prices, of course). We can serve chicken again at our dinner parties!

Indians eat a lot of chicken and have done so over the last few thousand years. Most restaurants sell tandoori chicken, chicken roasted in a clay oven, a relatively new dish from the northwest that swooped down to the rest of the nation starting in the late 1940s. But traditional curries have retained their hold. In western Goa, the curry may be cooked with garlic, onions, and a little bit of vinegar; in Bombay, with apricots; in northern cities like Delhi, with spinach and cardamom; in the east, it might be cooked in yogurt with cinnamon; and in the south with mustard seeds, curry leaves, and coconut milk.

Indians traditionally remove the skin before cooking either a whole chicken or chicken parts. They probably feel that spices penetrate better and that somehow the chicken is cleaner. I go both ways: sometimes I leave the skin on and sometimes I pull it off. It depends upon the recipe.

Hunters love their duck and quail. During the winter hunting season, these were invariably on our table at the start of each week after a busy weekend (men only) of *shikar*—the hunt. Game birds are either roasted with a coating of spices or slowly braised.

Soft-Boiled Eggs with Seasoned Salt

We all love these in our family.

Put the boiled eggs in egg cups, and have a saltcellar filled with seasoned salt on the side. I like to eat the eggs with toast cut into "soldiers"—long strips, perfect for dunking into the egg.

SERVES 1–2

2 eggs

FOR THE SEASONED SALT

1 tablespoon sea salt

Freshly ground pepper

½ teaspoon ground roasted cumin
    seeds (page 284)

Put enough water in a pan to cover the eggs and bring to a boil. Turn the heat down so the water is simmering gently. Lower the eggs into the water with the help of a spoon, one at a time. Set your timer for 4 minutes if you want the whites soft, 5–5½ minutes if you want the whites almost set, and 6 minutes if you want them completely set.

Meanwhile, mix the salt, pepper, and cumin together in a small bowl or saltcellar.

As soon as the eggs are done, remove them, put them in egg cups, and serve immediately.

Poached Eggs over Vegetables

I like to poach my eggs in a frying pan. I break them into the pan rather like fried eggs, laying them next to each other, only instead of oil, I use water. It is a much easier method. Then I serve them over well-spiced Indian vegetables, whatever I am in the mood for. I cook the vegetables in advance. Sometimes I use some leftover vegetables from the day before.

You may serve the eggs over Potatoes with Cumin and Mustard, Corn with Aromatic Seasonings, or Swiss Chard with Ginger and Garlic.

SERVES 2

4 eggs

Use a nonstick frying pan that will just hold 4 eggs with ease. A 9-inch pan is ideal, though one a little bit larger or smaller will do. Put about ¾ inch water in the pan and bring it to a low simmer. Break the eggs into the water so they lie side by side. Let them cook gently until the whites are almost set. Turn off the heat and cover very loosely. Allow the eggs to set to the consistency you like, watching them carefully. Separate the eggs and, using a slotted spatula, remove the eggs and place them directly on the chosen cooked vegetable.

A Two-Egg Masala Omelette

In our house, we all like different types of omelettes. We tend to make our own. This is how I make mine.

Indians generally eat their omelettes with sliced bread, toast, or *paratha*s.

SERVES 1

2 eggs, lightly beaten
Salt
Freshly ground black pepper
1 tablespoon olive or canola oil
$\frac{1}{8}$ teaspoon brown mustard seeds
$\frac{1}{16}$ teaspoon whole cumin seeds

1 teaspoon finely chopped shallots or red onions
3 cherry tomatoes, quartered
Dash of cayenne pepper or crushed red pepper
1 tablespoon finely chopped cilantro

Season the eggs lightly with salt and pepper.

Pour the oil into a 6- or 7-inch, preferably nonstick or other well-seasoned frying pan and set over medium-high heat. When hot, put in the mustard and cumin seeds. As soon as the mustard seeds pop, a matter of seconds, turn the heat to medium low. Toss in the shallots and stir them once or twice. Quickly add the tomatoes, cayenne, cilantro, and a dash of salt and pepper. Stir and cook about a minute or until the tomatoes have softened a bit. Stir the beaten eggs and add them, letting them spread out in the pan. Turn heat to medium. Quickly mix all the ingredients in the pan, and then let the mixture spread out to the edges of the pan. Cover until the eggs are almost set. Now fold the omelette, first bringing the left side slightly past the center and then the right side over the left side. Turn the omelette over, pressing down a bit with the spatula for a few seconds. Serve immediately.

Indian Scrambled Eggs

Here is our family's most beloved Sunday breakfast/brunch dish. I prepare all the ingredients beforehand and then scramble the eggs as we are sitting down to eat. Toast or heated flat-breads should be served on the side. I like to use the asafetida as it gives a truffle-like aroma, but you could leave it out if you wish.

You may have this with slices of French or Italian bread, with toast, or with any of the three Indian breads in this book.

SERVES 4–6

3 tablespoons olive or canola oil

$\frac{1}{16}$ teaspoon ground asafetida

$\frac{1}{4}$ teaspoon whole brown mustard seeds

$\frac{1}{4}$ teaspoon whole cumin seeds

1–2 teaspoons finely chopped fresh hot green chili

15–20 fresh curry leaves, if available, or 3 fresh basil leaves, torn up

4 medium-sized mushrooms, chopped small

1 tablespoon finely chopped red onions or shallots

2 teaspoons finely grated peeled fresh ginger

8–10 cherry tomatoes, chopped

3 tablespoons chopped cilantro

12 eggs, beaten

A scant $\frac{1}{2}$ teaspoon salt, or to taste

Freshly ground black pepper

Pour the oil into a large, preferably nonstick frying pan and set on medium-high heat. When hot, sprinkle in the asafetida and mustard and cumin seeds. As soon as the mustard seeds begin to pop, a matter of seconds, put in the chili, curry leaves, and mushrooms. Stir once or twice and put in the onions. Stir a few times and add the ginger and tomatoes. Stir a few times and add the cilantro, eggs, salt, and pepper. Turn heat to medium-low. Now just stir to mix and scramble the eggs to the doneness you like, always scraping from the bottom.

Egg Curry

Here is a very easy-to-prepare egg curry. As the entire curry sauce is made in the blender, I call it a blender curry. If you like, 2–3 medium-sized boiled and diced (a ¾-inch dice is best) potatoes may be added to the sauce at the same time as the eggs.

Serve with rice or any of the three breads in this book. You may also have the curry with French or Italian bread.

SERVES 4–6

4 tablespoons plain yogurt
4 medium tomatoes (about 1¼ pounds), chopped
3 tablespoons chickpea flour (also sold as gram flour or *besan*)
One 1-inch piece fresh ginger, peeled and chopped
3 teaspoons hot curry powder (I like Bolst's Hot Curry Powder)

1¼–1½ teaspoons salt
2 tablespoons olive or canola oil
½ teaspoon whole cumin seeds
½ teaspoon whole mustard seeds
¼ teaspoon whole fennel seeds
8–12 hard-boiled eggs, peeled and left whole

Pour 1 cup water, the yogurt, tomatoes, chickpea flour, ginger, curry powder, and salt into a blender in the order listed. Blend for at least 2 minutes or until you have a smooth sauce.

Put the oil into a wide pan and set over medium-high heat. When hot, put in the cumin and mustard seeds. As soon as the mustard seeds begin to pop, a matter of seconds, add the fennel seeds. Wait about 5 seconds and take the pan off the heat. Pour in 1 cup water and then the curry sauce from the blender. Stir and put the pan back on the heat, turning it to medium. Bring the sauce to a simmer, stirring all the time. Cover, turn heat to very low, and simmer gently for 15 minutes, stirring now and then. Add the hard-boiled eggs and heat them through.

Chicken Karhai with Mint

A *karhai* is an Indian wok (many anthropologists believe that the utensil actually originated in India), and this is a stir-fried dish. I like dark meat and prefer chicken thighs here, but lovers of white meat may use boned and skinned chicken breasts.

Serve it with rice or Indian (or Middle Eastern) flatbreads. You could serve the Mushroom and Pea Curry on the side. You could also have this cold, even take it on a picnic.

SERVES 4

FOR THE MARINADE

1¼ pounds boneless, skinless chicken thighs, cut into ¾-inch pieces
1 teaspoon salt
Freshly ground black pepper
½ teaspoon ground cumin seeds
1 teaspoon ground coriander seeds
1½ tablespoons lemon juice
½ teaspoon cayenne pepper
1 teaspoon *garam masala* (page 285)
1 teaspoon finely grated peeled fresh ginger
1 tablespoon olive or canola oil

YOU ALSO NEED

3 tablespoons olive or canola oil
¾ cup chopped onions
3 tablespoons chopped fresh mint

Combine all the ingredients listed in the marinade in a glass or stainless steel bowl. Mix, cover, and refrigerate for at least 30 minutes or as long as overnight.

Pour the 3 tablespoons of oil into a wok, *karhai,* or large frying pan and set over medium-high heat. When hot, add the onions. Stir-fry for a minute. Add the chicken with all its marinade. Stir-fry another 3 minutes or until the chicken is just cooked through. Add the mint and stir-fry a few seconds.

Stir-Fried Chettinad Chicken

A dish from the southeastern state of Tamil Nadu, this quick stir-fry has all the wonderful spices used in the cooking of the Chettiyars, a trading community—lots of black pepper, fennel seeds, mustard seeds, cinnamon, and the split pea, *urad dal.* (Yellow split peas may be substituted for the *urad dal.* They will be used here in a very southern way, as a seasoning.)

This dish has a 30-minute marinating period, but it cooks in about 7 minutes. It is a good idea to have all the spices measured out and ready, as the stir-frying is done quickly.

I like this chicken with Basmati Rice with Lentils and a green vegetable.

SERVES 4

1¼ pounds boned and skinned chicken thighs (if you prefer light meat, skinned and boned breasts may be substituted)

1 teaspoon salt

Freshly ground black pepper

1 teaspoon finely grated peeled fresh ginger

¼ teaspoon ground turmeric

¼ teaspoon cayenne pepper

4 tablespoons olive or canola oil

½ teaspoon whole brown mustard seeds

½ teaspoon skinned *urad dal* (use yellow split peas as a substitute)

½ teaspoon whole fennel seeds

Two 2-inch cinnamon sticks

2 dried hot red chilies

20 fresh curry leaves, if available, or 8 basil leaves, torn up

½ medium onion, chopped

8 cherry tomatoes, halved

Cut the chicken into ¾-inch pieces and put in a bowl. Add the salt, a very generous quantity of black pepper, the ginger, turmeric, and cayenne. Mix well, cover, and refrigerate 30 minutes.

Pour the oil into a wok or large frying pan and set over medium-high heat. When hot, put in the mustard seeds, *urad dal,* fennel seeds, cinnamon, and red chilies. As soon as the mustard seeds pop, a matter of seconds, put in the curry leaves, onions, and chicken. Stir and fry for about 5 minutes or until the chicken has cooked through and has browned. Add the tomatoes and stir for 30 seconds. Check for salt, adding a light sprinkling if needed.

Stir-Fried Chicken Breast
with Black Pepper and Green Chilies

I like to use bird's-eye chilies here, but any fresh hot green chilies will do. Use only as much of the larger chilies as you think you can handle. I often make this when I am in a hurry, as it cooks fast.

You could serve this with any rice dish. I like it with the Tomato Pullao. This is also great to take on picnics or serve at a summer lunch: fill pita bread pockets with this, spoon in a little Fresh Green Chutney, and eat!

SERVES 2–3

¾ pound boneless, skinless chicken breast, cut into ¾-inch pieces
1 clove garlic, crushed to a pulp
1 teaspoon very finely grated peeled fresh ginger
½ teaspoon salt
2 teaspoons lemon juice
A generous amount of freshly ground black pepper

⅛ teaspoon cayenne pepper
2 tablespoons vegetable oil
4 whole cardamom pods
½ medium onion, finely chopped
1–2 fresh hot bird's-eye chilies, chopped
2 tablespoons plain yogurt
⅛ teaspoon ground turmeric

Combine the chicken, garlic, ginger, salt, lemon juice, black pepper, and cayenne in a bowl. Mix well.

Put the oil in a frying pan or wok and set over medium-high heat. When hot, put in the cardamom pods. Stir once and put in the onions and chilies. Stir and fry until the onion pieces turn brown at the edges. Add 1 tablespoon yogurt and stir it until it disappears. Add the second tablespoon of yogurt. When it disappears, add the turmeric and the seasoned chicken. Stir and fry for a minute. Add 2 tablespoons water, cover, and turn heat to low. Cook 2 minutes or until the chicken is cooked through. Remove cover. Turn heat up and let all the liquid dry up, stirring as this happens.

Goan-Style Chicken Moelho

There is a whole family of Goan meat and chicken dishes that have in common the use of garlic, vinegar, and hot chilies—all of which help preserve the food and give it a slightly "pickled" feel. As in the case of the more famous *vindaloos,* the garlic and vinegar combination probably came from Portuguese culinary traditions—Goa was their colony for four hundred years or so. It was the Portuguese who introduced chilies to India in the late fifteenth century. Indians, already familiar with their own black pepper, took to them with a passion.

The chilies used in Goa are often of the Kashmiri variety, which give off a very red color but are of medium heat. Each dish requires rather a lot of them and ends up being very hot and very red. I have used a mixture of cayenne and paprika. You can add more cayenne if you like.

In Goa this is eaten with partially milled red-hulled rice. You could serve it with Plain Brown Rice, Plain Jasmine Rice, or Coconut Rice. Add vegetables and salads.

SERVES 3–4

1½ teaspoons whole cumin seeds

1 teaspoon whole brown mustard seeds

1¼ pound boneless, skinless chicken thighs, extra fat removed and cut into 1-inch pieces

¾–1 teaspoon cayenne pepper

2 teaspoons nice red paprika

½ teaspoon ground turmeric

1¼ teaspoons salt

1 tablespoon red wine vinegar, plus a little more, as needed

4 cloves garlic, crushed to a pulp with a garlic press

3 tablespoons olive or canola oil

1 medium onion (about 5 ounces) cut into fine half rings

Put the cumin seeds and mustard seeds into the container of a clean coffee grinder and grind finely.

Put the chicken in a nonreactive bowl along with the cumin-mustard mixture, cayenne, paprika, turmeric, salt, 1 tablespoon vinegar, and the garlic. Mix well with your hands, cover, and set aside for 1–2 hours, refrigerating if needed.

Pour the oil into a large, preferably nonstick frying pan and set over medium-high heat. When hot, put in the onions. Stir and fry until the onions turn translucent, about 4–5 minutes. Keep stirring and frying another 2 minutes or until the onions brown a bit. Now add all the marinated chicken. Stir and fry another 7–8 minutes or until the chicken turns opaque and browns a bit. Add ½ cup water and another 2 teaspoons vinegar. Bring to a boil. Cover, turn heat to low, and simmer gently for 5 minutes. Check the salt, adding more if needed.

Chicken with Okra

This very home-style Indian dish may best be compared to a New Orleans gumbo. It is the okra and tomatoes that give it the gumbo feel, but the seasonings are very North Indian.

Serve with rice or with Indian breads.

SERVES 2–3

1 pound boneless, skinless chicken
    thighs cut into 1–1½-inch pieces
2 teaspoons ground cumin
2 teaspoons ground coriander
½ teaspoon ground turmeric
½–¾ teaspoon cayenne pepper
Salt
1 tablespoon lemon juice

3 tablespoons olive or canola oil
½ teaspoon whole cumin seeds
1 medium onion, chopped
20 medium-sized okra, about 5 ounces,
    with tips and tops removed and
    each okra halved
1 medium tomato, peeled and chopped

Put the chicken in a nonreactive bowl. Add the cumin, coriander, turmeric, cayenne, 1 teaspoon salt, and lemon juice. Stir to mix well. Cover and refrigerate for 1–2 hours.

Pour the oil into a frying pan, preferably nonstick, and set it over medium-high heat. When hot, put in the cumin seeds, onions, and okra. Stir and fry 6–7 minutes or until the onions have browned a bit. Now put in all the marinated chicken. Stir and fry for 3–4 minutes or until the chicken pieces turn pale. (If some of the spices stick to the pan, do not worry.) Add ½ cup water, ¼ teaspoon salt, and the tomato. Stir to mix and bring to a simmer. Cover, turn heat to low, and simmer gently for 10 minutes.

Tandoori-Style Chicken with Mint

An 8–24-hour marination period is required here.

This chicken tastes just as good cold as it does hot, making it perfect for everyday meals, formal dinners, and picnics. (Once cooked, if properly wrapped and refrigerated, the chicken will hold for 5–6 days.)

SERVES 4

4 whole chicken legs (about 2¾ pounds), skinned and separated into drumsticks and thighs
1 teaspoon salt
2 tablespoons lemon juice
½ medium onion, chopped
3 cloves garlic, chopped
One 3-inch piece fresh ginger, peeled and chopped

½ teaspoon cayenne pepper
1 teaspoon *garam masala,* homemade (page 285) or store-bought
2 teaspoons ground cumin seeds
1 cup plain yogurt
3 tablespoons olive or canola oil or *ghee*
4 tablespoons finely chopped fresh mint

Cut 2 deep diagonal slits into the fleshy parts of each thigh and 2 diagonal slits into both fleshy sides of each drumstick. Put the chicken parts on a large plate in a single layer. Rub both sides first with the salt and then the lemon juice. Set aside for 20 minutes.

Meanwhile, put the onions, garlic, ginger, cayenne, *garam masala,* cumin, and yogurt into a blender and blend until you have a smooth paste. Put the chicken and all accumulated juices in a bowl. Add the paste from the blender and mix well. Cover and refrigerate overnight or 24 hours.

Preheat oven to 500°F.

Remove chicken from the marinade and lay the pieces in a single layer in a baking tray. Brush with oil and then sprinkle with half the mint. Bake 15 minutes. Turn the pieces over, brush with more oil, and sprinkle the remaining mint over the top. Bake another 5 minutes.

Chicken Roasted with Ginger and Cilantro

There is something about the combination of fresh ginger and cilantro that tastes very Indian, very Delhi, to me, very much like home. In India, where few people have ovens, the chicken is browned first with the spices in a pan and then cooked on top of the stove over a low flame. I have, over the years, mastered making it in the oven, only because it requires much less effort and the results are exactly the same.

This chicken may be served hot, with rice or breads (pita bread would be fine too), a green vegetable, and Black Beans served on the side, but it is also excellent when cold and perfect for picnics.

SERVES 4–5

$3\frac{1}{2}$ pounds chicken legs, separated into drumsticks and thighs (5 legs)

$1\frac{1}{2}$ teaspoons salt

Freshly ground black pepper, generous amounts

$\frac{1}{2}$ teaspoon cayenne pepper, or to taste

1 teaspoon *garam masala* (homemade is best, page 285, but store-bought will do)

1 teaspoon finely grated peeled fresh ginger

2 tablespoons plain yogurt, preferably the acidophilus variety sold in health-food stores

1 cup chopped fresh cilantro (do not use the coarser stems)

Preheat oven to 400°F.

Lay the chicken pieces in a single layer in a lasagna-type baking dish. Sprinkle the salt, pepper, cayenne, and *garam masala* evenly on both sides and pat in. Now rub the ginger, yogurt, and cilantro all over the pieces. Make sure that the chicken pieces end up skin-side down. Place the baking dish in the oven and bake 25 minutes. Turn the chicken pieces over. Continue to bake, basting with the pan juices every 10 minutes, until the chicken is cooked through and the top has browned, another 35 minutes.

Chicken with Spinach

Here is another of my party favorites, as it is quite easy to prepare and may be done ahead of time and reheated. I do all the
chopping in a food processor, which takes just a few minutes.
You may, if you prefer, chop the onions by hand and grate the
ginger finely and put the garlic through a garlic press. The
results will be the same. I have used fresh spinach only because
I grow so much of it; you may use frozen chopped spinach
instead.

For a dinner, I might serve this with Rice Pilaf with Almonds
and Raisins, Eggplants in a North-South Sauce, and a yogurt relish.

SERVES 6

6 chicken legs, separated into
    drumsticks and thighs, or any
    other chicken parts you like,
    about 4¼ pounds in all
Salt
Freshly ground black pepper
2 medium onions, coarsely cut up
One 2-inch piece fresh ginger, peeled
    and chopped
6 medium cloves garlic, coarsely
    chopped

1 tablespoon nice red paprika
½ teaspoon cayenne pepper
5 tablespoons olive or canola oil
Two 2-inch cinnamon sticks
8 whole cardamom pods
10 ounces spinach, chopped (frozen,
    defrosted, and lightly drained
    spinach may be used instead)

Spread the chicken out in a single layer and sprinkle 1 teaspoon salt and
lots of black pepper on both sides.

Put the onions, ginger, garlic, paprika, and cayenne into a food processor
and, using a fast start-and-stop method, chop all the ingredients as finely as
possible, stopping short of making a puree.

Put the oil into a wide, heavy pan (a large nonstick sauté pan or well-
seasoned wok is ideal) and set over medium-high heat. When hot, put in the

cinnamon and cardamom. Let them sizzle for a few seconds. Now put in as much chicken as will fit easily in a single layer, and brown on both sides. Remove to a bowl, leaving the whole spices behind. Brown all the chicken this way in batches. Then put the onion mixture into the pan, turning heat down to medium. Stir and fry for 4–5 minutes, until most of the liquid has dried up. Add the spinach and $\frac{1}{2}$ teaspoon salt. Stir and fry another 4–5 minutes. Add the chicken, $\frac{1}{4}$ teaspoon salt, and $\frac{1}{2}$ cup water, and bring to a boil. Cover, turn heat to low, and simmer gently for 25 minutes, turning the chicken pieces over gently a few times. Extra fat may be removed before serving.

Baked Chicken Curry

Here the chicken is marinated overnight with most of the ingredients needed and then baked in its marinating dish, magically creating a curry. If a slightly sweet taste is desired, 2 tablespoons of golden raisins may be added to the marinade.

Serve with rice and Green Lentils with Green Beans and Cilantro.

SERVES 4

2½ pounds chicken parts

1 teaspoon salt

Freshly ground black pepper

2 tablespoons lemon juice

2 teaspoons finely grated peeled fresh ginger

1 large clove garlic, crushed

5 tablespoons whole-milk yogurt

1½ tablespoons ground coriander

2 teaspoons ground cumin

½ teaspoon ground turmeric

½ teaspoon cayenne pepper

6 cardamom pods

2 tablespoons finely chopped red onions or shallots

A little oil for basting

Put the chicken in a casserole-type dish so it fits easily in a single layer. Add the salt, lots of black pepper, and the lemon juice. Mix well and set aside for 20 minutes.

Combine the ginger, garlic, yogurt, coriander, cumin, turmeric, cayenne, and cardamom in a bowl. Mix well. Rub the chicken with this mixture, cover, and refrigerate overnight.

Preheat oven to 400°F.

Bring the chicken to room temperature. Brush the top with oil and scatter the onions over the top. Place in the middle of the oven for 30 minutes. Turn the chicken pieces over and put back in the oven. Cook another 40 minutes, basting every 10 minutes with the juices.

Chicken Baked in a Packet

You could use any chicken parts you like for this recipe—dark meat, light meat, or a combination. The bones should stay in but the skin should be pulled off. This chicken needs to be marinated for at least 4 hours.

Serve with Plain Basmati Rice, My Everyday Moong Dal, Spinach with Garlic and Cumin, a yogurt relish, and a salad to get the feel of a simple family meal in North India.

SERVES 2–4

1 teaspoon ground coriander

1 teaspoon ground cumin

2 teaspoons bright red paprika

$\frac{1}{4}$–$\frac{1}{2}$ teaspoon cayenne pepper

$\frac{1}{2}$ teaspoon ground turmeric

2 cloves garlic, crushed in a garlic press

$1\frac{1}{2}$ teaspoons finely grated peeled
fresh ginger

3 tablespoons whole-milk yogurt

2 teaspoons lemon juice

1 teaspoon salt

Freshly ground black pepper

$1\frac{1}{2}$ pounds chicken parts, skinned

Combine the coriander, cumin, paprika, cayenne, turmeric, garlic, ginger, yogurt, lemon juice, salt, and pepper in a bowl. Mix to make a paste.

Spread a 24-inch piece of foil in front of you. Cut deep slits on the fleshy sides of the meat pieces, staying away from the edges. Lay the pieces side by side in a single row in the center of the foil. Rub the spice paste all over the chicken, going deep into the slits. Fold the top of the foil over the chicken, then the bottom, and, finally, the two sides. Refrigerate the packet at least 4 hours or overnight.

Preheat over to 400°F.

Place the chicken packet on a baking tray and bake for 30 minutes. Open the packet carefully and turn the chicken pieces over, basting with the juices. Close packet again and bake another 15 minutes.

Bangladeshi White Chicken Korma

I had this dish in Bangladesh and thought it was exquisite. It seemed to have come straight from the palaces of seventeenth-century Moghul rulers. It was a true *korma*, a stew cooked in yogurt, mild but exquisitely seasoned, and without any brown, yellow, or red spices to mar its pallor. There were some New World sliced green chilies scattered over the top, but they seemed a later addition. I have put them in—but even without them, the flavors are beyond compare. Of course, it helps to get a good-quality organic chicken. Have your butcher skin it and cut it into small serving pieces for you.

In Bangladesh, this chicken was cooked in *ghee* (clarified butter, page 286). I generally cook in oil. I like to use a good sour yogurt here, such as the acidophilus yogurt I get from the health-food store. If you cannot get that, just add 1 tablespoon lemon juice to the ordinary supermarket yogurt.

Serve this with rice or flatbreads or even in a Western way with potatoes and a vegetable.

SERVES 4

4 tablespoons olive or canola oil or *ghee*

Three 2-inch cinnamon sticks

3 bay leaves

10 cardamom pods

1 medium onion, sliced into fine half rings

One 3¾-pound chicken, skinned and cut into small serving pieces (breast into 6 pieces, each leg into 2 pieces, wings into 3 pieces, back into 3 pieces, neck into 2 pieces)

½ medium onion, chopped very finely

3 tablespoons finely grated peeled fresh ginger (use a fine microplane)

6 cloves garlic, crushed to a pulp with a garlic press

½ cup acidophilus yogurt, or plain yogurt plus 1 tablespoon lemon juice, beaten until smooth

1¼ teaspoons salt

1–2 teaspoons finely chopped fresh hot green chilies

Put the oil into a large sauté pan or a large, deep frying pan and set over medium-high heat. When the oil is really hot, put in the cinnamon, bay leaves, and cardamom. Stir for 10 seconds as the spices sizzle. Add the sliced onions. Stir and fry for about 3 minutes or until the onions brown a bit. Add the chicken pieces. Stir and cook 5–6 minutes or until the chicken pieces brown lightly. Add the chopped onions, the ginger, and the garlic. Stir and fry for 2 minutes. Add the yogurt and salt. Stir and cook for 10 minutes. Add the chilies and 3 tablespoons water. Bring to a simmer. Cover, turn heat to low, and simmer very gently for another 10–15 minutes or until the chicken is tender.

Kerala-Style Chicken Curry

Here is a creamy, coconut-enriched chicken curry that takes me back to the balmy southwest breezes of Kerala's palm-lined coast.

Serve with Plain Jasmine Rice and a green vegetable.

3 tablespoons olive or canola oil

$\frac{1}{2}$ teaspoon whole cumin seeds

$\frac{1}{2}$ teaspoon whole brown mustard seeds

One 5-ounce onion, cut in half lengthways and then crossways into fine half rings

2 teaspoons finely grated peeled fresh ginger

4 cloves garlic, chopped finely

$2\frac{1}{2}$ pounds chicken parts, skinned

$\frac{1}{2}$ teaspoon cayenne pepper, or more, if desired

1 tablespoon bright red paprika

1 teaspoon salt

15–20 fresh curry leaves, if available, or 8 fresh basil leaves, torn up

1 cup coconut milk from a well-shaken can

3 or 4 whole bird's-eye chilies (optional)

Put the oil into a wide pan and set over medium-high heat. When hot, put in the cumin and mustard seeds. As soon as the mustard seeds begin to pop, a matter of seconds, add the onions. Stir and fry until the onions have browned lightly. Add the ginger, garlic, chicken, cayenne, paprika, salt, and curry leaves. Stir for a minute. Add 1 cup water and bring to a simmer. Cover, lower heat, and simmer gently for 25 minutes, stirring now and then. Boil down most of the liquid. Add the coconut milk and, if using, float the whole bird's-eye chilies on top, and cook, stirring on medium-high heat for a minute.

Chicken Curry with Cardamom

A gentle, family-style curry.

   If you leave out the cayenne pepper, this may even be served to small children, along with rice and perhaps Corn with Aromatic Seasonings.

5 tablespoons olive or canola oil
Two 2-inch cinnamon sticks
8 cardamom pods
One 3½-pound chicken, cut up into
   10–12 serving pieces
2 cups chopped onions
2 cloves garlic, finely chopped
2 tablespoons ground coriander

1 tablespoon ground cumin
¼ teaspoon ground turmeric
½ teaspoon cayenne pepper, or to taste
2 medium tomatoes, chopped
4 cups chicken stock
Salt

Pour the oil into a large, wide sauté pan and turn heat to high. When hot, put in the cinnamon and cardamom. Ten seconds later, put in as many chicken pieces as will fit easily and brown them until golden on all sides. Remove to a bowl, leaving the whole spices behind in the pan. Brown the remaining chicken the same way, removing pieces to a bowl. Add the onions to the pan, turning heat down to medium, and sauté them until they start to brown lightly at the edges. Add the garlic and stir a few times. Now add the coriander, cumin, turmeric, and cayenne. Stir once or twice. Put in the tomatoes. Stir them until they begin to soften. Return the browned chicken and all accumulated juices to the pan, along with the chicken stock, ½ teaspoon salt if the stock is salted, 1 teaspoon if it is not, and bring to a boil. Cover, turn heat to medium, and cook somewhat rapidly for 15 minutes. Remove cover and turn heat to high. Cook, stirring now and then, until only a thick sauce remains.

OVERLEAF, LEFT: *Kerala-Style Chicken Curry*
RIGHT: *My Everyday Moong Dal*

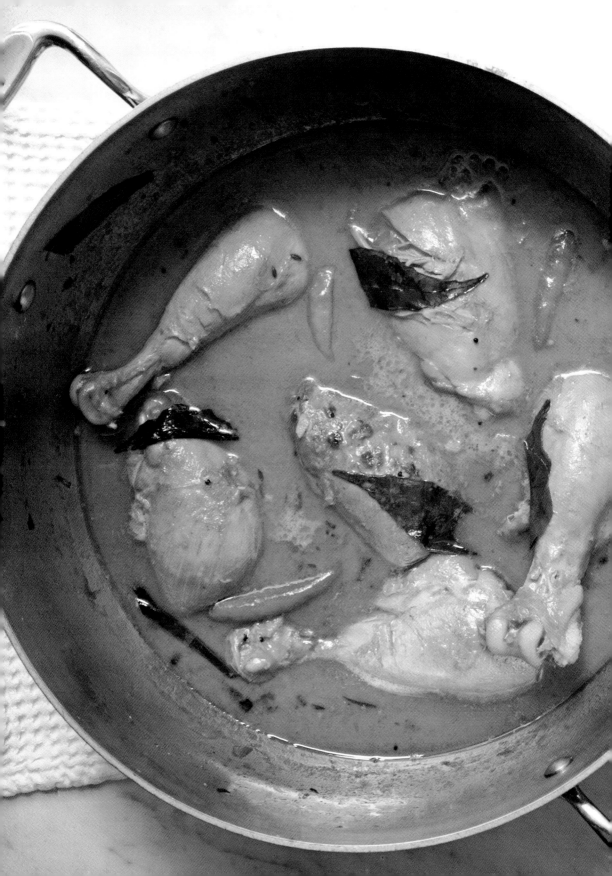

Chicken with Vindaloo Spices

Vindaloo implies garlic and vinegar, and this dish certainly has plenty of both. Make it as hot as you like. The heat balances the tartness.

This dish holds well and, because it does not have too much sauce, is wonderful to take on picnics.

SERVES 4

4 tablespoons olive or canola oil

$\frac{1}{2}$ teaspoon whole brown mustard seeds

$\frac{1}{4}$ teaspoon whole fenugreek seeds

1 teaspoon whole black peppercorns

15–20 fresh curry leaves or 10 fresh basil leaves, torn up

8 chicken thighs

6 cloves garlic, chopped

1 cup apple cider vinegar or white wine vinegar

$1\frac{1}{4}$ teaspoons salt

$1\frac{1}{2}$ teaspoons ground cumin seeds

1 tablespoon ground coriander seeds

$\frac{1}{2}$–1 teaspoon cayenne pepper, or more if you wish

1 tablespoon bright red paprika

Pour the oil into a very wide pot, large sauté pan, or wide frying pan—anything large enough to hold the chicken in a single layer. Set over medium-high heat. When hot, put in the mustard seeds. As soon as they pop, a matter of seconds, put in the fenugreek seeds and peppercorns. A few seconds later add the curry leaves, chicken, and all the remaining ingredients. Stir and bring to a boil. Cover, turn heat to low, and simmer gently for 20 minutes. Remove the cover, turn heat to high, and cook, stirring and turning, until all the liquid evaporates and the chicken browns on all sides.

Chicken with Apricots

The Parsi community of India is of Persian descent. When the Parsis fled Iran in the tenth century, they settled on India's west coast, where they managed to preserve not only their religious traditions—they are Zoroastrians—but many of their culinary traditions as well. This delicately sweet-and-sour dish of chicken cooked with dried apricots is part of that tradition. I have a Parsi friend who puts in a healthy glug of Madeira toward the end of the cooking. Parsis picked up many customs not only from their Gujarati neighbors but also from their neighbors and masters in nineteenth-century Bombay, the British.

This dish is generally served with a mountain of very fine, crisp potato straws—you can just buy a large packet of them—but may also be served with rice.

SERVES 4

About 2½ pounds chicken (I use 8 thighs or drumsticks or a mixture of the two, but a cut-up chicken would be fine)
Salt
Freshly ground black pepper
12 dried apricots, preferably the nice orange Turkish ones
3 tablespoons olive or canola oil
Two 2-inch cinnamon sticks
½ teaspoon whole cumin seeds

2 medium onions, cut into fine half rings
3 teaspoons finely grated peeled fresh ginger
1 tablespoon tomato paste
1½ tablespoons sugar
2 tablespoons red wine vinegar
1 teaspoon *garam masala*, preferably homemade (page 285) but store-bought will do
½–¾ teaspoon cayenne pepper

Sprinkle the chicken on all sides with ½ teaspoon salt and very generous amounts of black pepper. Pat in and set aside.

Put the apricots in a small pan with 1 cup water and bring to a boil. Lower heat and gently simmer for about 15 minutes or until apricots have softened but are firm enough to take another 5 minutes of cooking later. Leave in the cooking liquid.

Pour the oil into a large frying pan or sauté pan and set over medium-high heat. When hot, scatter in the cinnamon sticks and cumin. Ten seconds later, put in half of the chicken pieces and brown them on both sides. Remove to a bowl. Put the remaining chicken pieces in the frying pan and brown them the same way, then remove to the bowl. Add the onions to the oil in the pan. Stir and fry them until they turn brown at the edges. Add the ginger and stir for a few seconds. Add the tomato paste and stir once. Now return the chicken and all accumulated juices to the pan, along with 1½ cups water and 1 teaspoon salt. Cover and bring to a boil. Lower heat and cook gently for 15 minutes, turning the chicken once during this period. Remove cover and add the sugar, vinegar, apricots and their cooking liquid, *garam masala,* and cayenne. Stir gently and cook on high heat until the sauce is a bit syrupy, about 5 minutes.

Whole Chicken Baked
with an Almond and Onion Sauce

This is an oven-cooked version of the Indian classic Murgh Mussallam—a whole chicken cooked in a rich spicy sauce. Although Indians like their chicken skinned, partly to let the spices penetrate better, I have not bothered too much with that in this book, just to make life easier. But it would be good to do it for this recipe, as this is a dish for special occasions. You can ask your butcher to skin the chicken, but it is really not difficult to yank most of it off yourself. The wings are a bit troublesome, so I just leave them alone.

I might go to town here and serve Black Beans, Yellow Basmati Rice with Sesame Seeds, and Sweet-and-Sour Eggplant. On the other hand, you could treat this as a spicy roast and just have parsley potatoes and fresh summer peas!

SERVES 4

FOR THE SPICE PASTE

2 tablespoons lemon juice

1 cup plain yogurt

1 medium onion, chopped

One 3-inch piece fresh ginger, peeled and chopped

3 large cloves garlic, chopped

¾ teaspoon cayenne pepper

1¾ teaspoons salt

2 teaspoons *garam masala* (preferably homemade, page 285)

2 tablespoons slivered blanched almonds

YOU ALSO NEED

1 whole chicken, about 3¾ pounds

½ teaspoon salt

1 tablespoon lemon juice

3 tablespoons olive or canola oil

½ teaspoon whole cumin seeds

Put all the ingredients for the paste in a blender in the order listed and blend to a smooth paste.

Remove as much of the chicken skin as you can easily. Cut 2–3 deep diagonal gashes in the fleshy part of each breast and thigh. Rub ½ teaspoon salt and 1 tablespoon lemon juice all over the chicken, inside and out. Leave for 15 minutes. Now put the chicken in a bowl. Spread the spice paste all over, cover, and refrigerate 4–24 hours.

Preheat oven to 400°F.

Pour the oil into a large, flame- and ovenproof casserole pan large enough to enclose the chicken and set over medium-high heat. When hot, put in the cumin seeds. Let them sizzle for 10 seconds and then put in the whole chicken, breast up, as well as all the marinade. Bring to a simmer. Cover, and place the pan with the chicken in the oven. Bake for 30 minutes. Uncover. Bake uncovered another 40 minutes or so, basting with the sauce every 10 minutes, until the chicken is tender.

Turkey Chappali Kebabs

Chappali kebabs, popular throughout much of Pakistan but originating near its borders with Afghanistan, are beef patties shallow-fried in the fat rendered from the tail of a fat-tailed sheep. If you can imagine a juicy, spicy hamburger cooked in roast beef drippings, you get a general idea: delicious but iffy on the health front. So over the years, I have come up with my own version, a turkey kebab.

I serve these kebabs with Thin Raw Onion Rings and the local Peshawari Red Pepper Chutney. You may even put this kebab in a hamburger bun, along with the onion rings and either a good squirt of lemon juice or some tomato ketchup.

MAKES 6 PATTIES

2 tablespoons plain yogurt
1 pound ground turkey (preferably a
    mixture of light and dark meat)
¾ teaspoon salt, or to taste
1 tablespoon whole coriander seeds
    and 1 teaspoon whole cumin seeds,
    crushed lightly in a mortar or put
    between sheets of foil and crushed
    with a rolling pin

¼ cup finely chopped fresh mint
½ teaspoon crushed red pepper flakes
1 teaspoon finely grated peeled fresh
    ginger
5 tablespoons olive or canola oil

Spoon the yogurt into a small sieve and set it over a cup to drain. Ten minutes will do it, but longer will not hurt.

Now put this drained yogurt and all the ingredients *except the oil* in a bowl and mix well. Cover and refrigerate at least 1 hour or as long as 24 hours so flavors meld.

Divide the meat into six portions and form balls. Flatten the balls to make six 3½-inch clean-edged patties.

Pour the oil into a large frying pan and set over medium-high heat. When hot, put in as many patties as will fit in easily and fry about 1 minute or less on each side or until browned. Turn the heat down to medium low and continue to cook the patties, turning frequently, until the juices run clear when the patties are pressed. Make all the patties this way and serve hot.

Ground Turkey with Hyderabadi Seasonings

This dish may also be made with ground lamb, or, for that matter, with ground beef. When using turkey, make sure your butcher includes both light and dark meat. White meat alone will be very dry.

In Hyderabad, in the very center of South India, this *keema* (the Indian word for ground meat) is typically served at Sunday brunches with *khichri* (the dish of rice and split peas from which the British kedgeree was derived; see Rice with Moong Dal, page 213), *pappadom* for crunch, and pickles for pizzazz. Store-bought Indian pickles such as mango, lemon, or chili will do, but if you prefer, a sweeter preserved chutney would be just fine.

SERVES 4

3 tablespoons olive or canola oil

1 teaspoon whole mustard seeds

1 teaspoon whole cumin seeds

2 dried hot red chilies

10 fresh curry leaves, or 5 fresh basil leaves, torn up

½ cup finely chopped onions

2 cloves garlic, crushed in a garlic press

2 teaspoons finely grated peeled fresh ginger

1 pound ground turkey, dark and light meat combined

1 tablespoon ground coriander seeds

1 teaspoon ground cumin seeds

4 tablespoons plain yogurt

1 cup peas, fresh or frozen and defrosted

1 teaspoon salt

Pour the oil into a frying pan and set over medium-high heat. When hot, put in the mustard seeds, the cumin seeds, and the red chilies. As soon as the mustard seeds begin to pop, a matter of seconds, add the curry leaves and the onions. Stir and fry until the onion pieces turn brown at the edges. Add the garlic and ginger. Stir for half a minute. Add the ground turkey. Turn heat to medium. Stir as you break up all the lumps in the meat. Add the coriander, cumin, yogurt, and ½ cup water. Stir and bring to a boil. Cover, turn heat to low, and cook 35 minutes. Add the peas, salt, and ¼ cup water. Stir to mix. Cover and cook another 7–10 minutes.

Tandoori-Style Duck Breasts

These duck breasts are not cooked in a *tandoor*, and not even in an oven, but they do taste like *tandoor*-baked poultry, hence their name. I marinate them in the same manner that I would a tandoori chicken, then I quickly pan-fry them so they stay a little rare inside. They take just minutes to cook. As for the skin, which is flabby if not crisped to perfection—well, I just remove it entirely.

I like to serve this duck with Sri Lankan Rice with Cilantro and Lemon Grass and Swiss Chard with Ginger and Garlic.

SERVES 4

FOR THE MARINADE

1 tablespoon lemon juice
2 tablespoons plain yogurt
$\frac{1}{2}$ medium onion, chopped
2 cloves garlic, chopped
One 2-inch piece of fresh ginger, peeled
  and chopped
$\frac{1}{4}$ teaspoon cayenne pepper
$1\frac{1}{4}$ teaspoon salt
$\frac{1}{2}$ teaspoon ground turmeric
1 teaspoon *garam masala,* preferably
  homemade (page 285)

YOU ALSO NEED

The breasts of two ducks, about
  2 pounds in all
1 tablespoon olive or canola oil

Put the ingredients for the marinade in a blender in the listed order and blend until smooth.

Pull off the duck skin. Pat the breasts with paper towels until dry. Rub the marinade on both sides of each piece and put in a bowl. Cover and refrigerate at least 6 hours or overnight.

Pick up one breast. Most of the marinade will drop off, and some will still cling to the meat. That is all you want. Put the breast flat on a board and cut it crossways, holding the knife at a slight diagonal, into ⅓-inch-thick slices. Cut all the duck pieces this way.

Just before eating, set a large, heavy (preferably cast-iron) frying pan over medium-high heat. Let it get very hot. Brush it with oil. Now lay down about 8 slices of duck on the hot pan. As soon as they are lightly browned, a matter of seconds, turn them over and quickly brown the second side. Remove to a warm plate and cover loosely. Do all the slices this way and serve hot.

Pakistani Bhuna Quail

South Asians love their quail, which is generally brought home by hunters. I know that when the men in our family returned from their winter shoots, what I most looked forward to eating were not the larger creatures, the deer and the geese, but the smaller ones, the duck, partridge, and quail. Here is a quick, stir-fried (*bhuna* implies stirring and browning) version of a dish I had in Lahore, Pakistan.

This recipe may be easily doubled. Use a very large frying pan if you do so.

When eating quail—and you have to use your fingers—it is hard to think of any other food, even though rice, vegetables, other meats, and legumes are nearly always part of the meal.

SERVES 2

1 medium tomato, chopped
1 large clove garlic, chopped
One ½-inch piece fresh ginger, peeled
   and chopped
1 medium shallot, chopped
¾ teaspoon salt

½ teaspoon *garam masala,* homemade
   (page 285) or store-bought
¼ teaspoon cayenne pepper
¼ teaspoon ground turmeric
2 quail, split lengthways
2 tablespoons olive or canola oil
4 cardamom pods

Put the tomato, garlic, ginger, shallots, salt, *garam masala*, cayenne, and turmeric in a blender and blend until smooth. Pour into a bowl. Add the quail. Mix well and leave to marinate, covered, 2–4 hours in the refrigerator.

Pour the oil into a frying pan and set over medium-high heat. When hot, put in the cardamom pods. Ten seconds later, empty the contents of the bowl into the frying pan and bring to a boil. Cover, turn heat to medium, and cook about 10 minutes or until most of the liquid has evaporated. Remove cover. Now stir and brown the spice paste and quail, sprinkling the pan with water every time the spices seem to be catching. Keep doing this for about 5 minutes. By this time the quail should be lightly browned and cooked through and the spices, also browned, should form a thick paste around it.

OVERLEAF: *Grilling Lamb Kebabs*

Lamb, Pork, and Beef

Contrary to what many people in the West assume, a good 70 percent of Indians eat meat. They may not be able to afford to eat it every day or to buy it for lunch *and* dinner, but they eat it all the same, and with relish.

Several methods of cooking it have come down from ancient times when game was roasted on skewers and spits, pork was slowly braised in barely bubbling pots, beef was stir-fried in *karhai*s (woks) with aromatic spices, goat chops were stewed gently in coconut milk in the south and in milk in northern Kashmir, and lamb was cooked in packets of banana leaves.

Indians have adapted most of these methods to newer appliances such as electric stoves and grills, which are quite common in middle-class and upper-class homes (and that means more than three hundred million people). There are diehards, however, who, while they are wealthy enough to afford simple stoves, still insist that Indian foods taste best when cooked over wood—so some old traditions continue apace. I know a few of these diehards—most have a servant who does the cooking and the scrubbing of the blackened pots!

This chapter contains a range of dishes, from grilled meats to braised pot roasts. To make each of them successfully, the cut of meat is important.

WHAT KIND OF MEAT TO USE FOR CURRIES

Lamb In India and its neighboring countries, most curries are made with goat meat with bone attached. Most shoppers choose a bit of neck, a bit of shoulder, and a bit of shank meat and marrow bone, sometimes a bit of rib as well. The bones give a depth to the sauce. Most Westerners cannot deal with bones, and goat is harder to find and not a common choice. So I have used boneless lamb for most of my recipes. But what part of the lamb? All butchers want to sell you leg meat, as it is the most convenient for them. It is fine to use, but the texture is drier. I like the texture of shoulder meat, but even the butcher closest to me, from a very prestigious shop, does not carry it. Here is the ideal solution: find a butcher that does carry lamb shoulder. Then buy the whole shoulder and have the butcher cut it into boneless cubes for curry, about 1–1½-inch pieces. Save the bones for soups and stock and divide the meat into convenient packets that you can use, now and in the future. Freeze what you do not want to cook immediately.

Beef Hindus in India generally do not eat beef (it was not cooked in our Delhi kitchen, though we were free to eat it outside the home in hotels and restaurants), but Christians and Muslims in India, Pakistan, Bangladesh, and Sri Lanka cook it frequently. Use the cuts my recipes suggest.

Pork It is mostly the Christians of South Asia who love pork, though very often Hindus will eat it too. In the formerly Portuguese colony of Goa, every part of the pig is eaten, from ears to tails. Use the parts my recipes suggest. (No ears and tails, I promise!)

KEBABS

South Asians, especially those of the meat-eating fraternity, love their kebabs. This is especially true in my community, where we were always known as *sharabi-kebabis*—drinkers and eaters, "kebab" here standing for all good food. Kebabs are the ideal accompaniment for drinks, are easy first courses (at Kashmiri banquets, they sit atop hillocks of basmati rice at the very start of the meal), and, in countries like Pakistan, can have whole meals built around them.

They may be made out of cubed meat or ground meat. They may be cooked on skewers or slapped onto hot stones or griddles or even baked. In Bangladesh, leftover ground-meat kebabs are crumbled into the next day's *dal* to give it special flavor.

Even though India has an ancient history of both roasted and grilled meats, the kebab—even the word itself—owes its origins to the Arab world, where the simplest kebabs were cubes of lamb, marinated in olive oil and garlic, skewered, and then grilled. When Muslim invaders from the north first came into India in the tenth and eleventh centuries, they brought the concept of their kebabs with them. But India had no olive oil. All we had was mustard oil, which also has a strong flavor and aroma. We can only deduce that they must have substituted one for the other, as many kebab dishes in Pakistan and northern India have a touch of mustard oil in them.

Punjabi Lamb Kebabs

This is a basic Indian kebab recipe that has probably not changed much since the sixteenth century except for the addition of chilies and what is now the ubiquitous *chaat masala,* a mixture of hot and sour spices that most Indians just buy in the market. The use of mustard oil is interesting—I have seen it used for kebabs in both India and Pakistan. Both countries have a Punjab, as that state, today on India's western border and Pakistan's eastern border, was split into two when the British partitioned India.

Chaat masala can be bought at any Indian grocery. It is a spice mixture containing sour mango powder, roasted cumin, cayenne, and other seasonings. It adds a spicy sourness but is not essential. Just sprinkle a dash of cayenne, and some roasted ground cumin seeds, if available, over the top and add some squirts of lime juice.

I like to have these with Rice Pilaf with Almonds and Raisins and Sweet-and-Sour Eggplant.

SERVES 4–6

¾ cup whole-milk yogurt (preferably Greek)

6 tablespoons mustard oil or extra virgin olive oil

1¼ teaspoons salt

1 teaspoon cayenne pepper

2 cloves garlic, crushed to a pulp

2 teaspoons finely grated peeled fresh ginger

2 teaspoons *garam masala* (store-bought is fine)

2½ pounds boneless lamb from the leg, cut into 1-inch cubes

3 tablespoons melted butter

1 teaspoon store-bought *chaat masala,* or see suggestion above

Put the yogurt in a cloth-lined colander set in the sink. Leave 10–15 minutes. Put the drained yogurt in a bowl. Add the oil, salt, cayenne, garlic, ginger, and *garam masala* and beat well with a whisk to mix. Add the meat and mix again. Cover and refrigerate overnight or as long as 24 hours.

Preheat broiler.

Push 4 skewers through the centers of the lamb cubes, dividing them up equally. Leave the marinade behind. Brush generously with the melted butter. Rest the two ends of each skewer on the rim of a broiling tray (the tray catches the drips and the kebabs stay in suspension) and place the tray about 5 inches from the source of heat. Broil 5–7 minutes on the first side and another 5–7 minutes on the opposite or until the kebabs are done to your taste. Sprinkle the *chaat masala* over the top.

Punjabi Lamb Kebabs

Lamb Kebabs with Mint

Apart from serving these kebabs, freshly grilled and hot, at mealtimes, when they are always popular, I find that if I refrigerate the cooked kebabs overnight and then put them into a hamper for a picnic, they are equally loved outdoors and hold well. In fact, if properly wrapped and refrigerated, they will hold for a good 5–6 days, making them perfect for an impromptu cold meal. For a hot meal, serve with a rice dish and Indian vegetables. For a picnic, serve with salads and crusty French bread.

SERVES 4–6

6 tablespoons plain yogurt
1 tablespoon lemon juice
$1\frac{1}{4}$ teaspoons salt
$\frac{1}{2}$ teaspoon cayenne pepper
2 teaspoons ground cumin
2 teaspoons ground coriander
$\frac{1}{2}$ medium onion, chopped

One 1-inch piece fresh ginger, peeled and chopped
$2\frac{1}{2}$ pounds boneless lamb from the leg, cut into 1-inch cubes
3–4 tablespoons finely chopped fresh mint
Oil for brushing over the top

Combine the yogurt, lemon juice, salt, cayenne, cumin, coriander, onions, and ginger in a blender. Blend until you have a smooth paste.

Put the lamb in a nonreactive bowl and pour the paste from the blender over the top. Mix well and prod the lamb cubes with a fork. Cover and refrigerate overnight or as long as 24 hours.

Preheat broiler.

Push 4 skewers through the centers of the lamb cubes, dividing them up equally. Leave the marinade behind. Brush with oil and sprinkle mint all over. If you plan to broil rather than grill, rest the two ends of each skewer on the rim of a broiling tray (the tray catches the drips and the kebabs stay in suspension) and place the tray about 5 inches from the source of heat. Broil 5–7 minutes on the first side and another 5–7 minutes on the opposite or until the kebabs are done to your taste. Or grill over hot coals, turning once, until brown on all sides.

Lemony Ground Lamb with Mint and Cilantro

You need a fair amount of the fresh mint and cilantro here so the meat really tastes both lemony and herbal. The ginger adds to the fresh, cleansing feeling.

Serve with flatbreads or rice. For a snack, this ground meat, or *keema,* may be rolled up in flatbreads along with finely sliced shallots, chopped tomatoes, and, if you like, chopped fresh hot green chilies. Today, in the Western world, this would be called a "wrap." As children we wrapped this *keema* in a *chapati* (a whole-wheat flatbread) and my mother called it a *batta.*

SERVES 3–4

2 tablespoons olive or canola oil

Two 2-inch cinnamon sticks

¼ cup chopped onion

1 pound ground lamb (not too fatty)

2 teaspoons very finely grated peeled fresh ginger

¾ teaspoon salt

½ teaspoon cayenne pepper, or to taste

¼ cup finely chopped fresh mint (just the leaves)

¼ cup finely chopped cilantro (use the tops)

2 tablespoons lemon juice

¾ teaspoon *garam masala* (homemade, page 285)

Pour the oil into a large frying pan and set over medium-high heat. When hot, put in the cinnamon sticks. Let them sizzle for a few seconds. Add the onions. Stir and fry until the onion pieces turn brown at the edges. Now add the lamb and ginger. Stir and fry for about 5 minutes, breaking up the chunks of meat as you do so. Add 1 cup water, the salt, and cayenne. Stir and bring to a simmer. Cover, turn heat to low, and simmer gently for 30–40 minutes or until the meat is tender. Add the mint, cilantro, lemon juice, and *garam masala.* Stir and cook uncovered on low heat for another 5 minutes, stirring now and then. Spoon out extra fat before serving.

Ground Lamb with Potatoes

Our family eats this so frequently that, along with a *moong dal,* rice, a yogurt relish, and pickles, we consider this to be our "soul food" meal. Nothing fancy here, only the homey and soothing.

SERVES 4–6

3 tablespoons olive or canola oil

Two 3-inch cinnamon sticks

1 medium onion, finely chopped

1 teaspoon finely grated peeled fresh ginger

3 cloves garlic, finely chopped

2 pounds ground lamb

3 tablespoons plain yogurt

3 tablespoons tomato puree

1 teaspoon ground cumin

2 teaspoons ground coriander

$\frac{1}{4}$ teaspoon cayenne pepper

$\frac{1}{4}$ teaspoon ground turmeric

$1\frac{3}{4}$ teaspoons salt

10 ounces boiling potatoes, peeled and cut into $\frac{3}{4}$-inch cubes

Pour the oil into a large frying pan or sauté pan and set over medium-high heat. When hot put in the cinnamon sticks and let them sizzle for 5 seconds. Put in the onions and stir and fry until the onion pieces turn brown at the edges. Add the ginger and garlic and stir for a minute. Add the lamb. Stir and fry, breaking up the lumps until the meat loses its redness. Add the yogurt, tomato puree, cumin, coriander, cayenne, and turmeric and stir for a minute. Add the salt, potatoes, and 2 cups water. Stir and bring to a boil. Cover, turn heat to low, and cook gently for 30 minutes.

Pakistani-Style Grilled Lamb Chops

When I was in Pakistan last, there was a very successful grill house in Karachi serving a thousand people per night. Bar-B-Q Tonight, as it was called, offered all manner of meats grilled in a style that is a mixture of Afghan and Pakistani culinary traditions. I have adapted one of their goat meat recipes to lamb. You may use the smaller rib chops or the larger, steak-like shoulder chops. They will have bone, of course, so 2 pounds will serve 2–3 people. You can cook these on an outdoor grill instead of broiling. This recipe may also be used for beef steaks.

I love this with Tomato Pullao and Pan-Grilled Zucchini. I make the rice first and let it sit wrapped up in a towel while I grill the kebabs and the zucchini.

SERVES 2–3

4 teaspoons very finely grated peeled fresh ginger
2 teaspoons garlic, crushed to a pulp
1 tablespoon lemon juice
1¼ teaspoons salt
½–¾ teaspoon cayenne pepper
Freshly ground black pepper

½ teaspoon *garam masala*, preferably homemade (page 285), but store-bought is fine
2 pounds lamb chops, shoulder or rib
2 tablespoons mustard, olive, or canola oil

Combine the ginger, garlic, lemon juice, salt, cayenne, black pepper, and *garam masala* in a shallow dish large enough to hold the chops. Mix well. Rub this marinade on both sides of the chops, cover, and refrigerate 4–24 hours.

Just before eating, preheat the broiler and set a rack 4–5 inches from the source of heat.

Put the chops, with any marinade that clings to them easily, in a baking tray, brush both sides with oil, and place under broiler. Broil 3–4 minutes on each side or until browned. If the chops are an inch thick they will still be pink inside, the way I like them. If you want them more done, put them in a 350°F oven for 5–10 minutes, depending on the thickness of the chops and the doneness desired.

Delhi-Style Bhuna Lamb

Bhuna means "browned"—actually, the process of browning. So in this dish the meat has a browned look to it, and whatever sauce there is, it is thick and clings to the meat. This is a family recipe that comes via my niece, Abha. If you like, two slit hot green chilies may be added at the same time as the cilantro, just before the final stir.

I like to eat this with Indian flatbreads (pita or other store-bought flatbreads may be substituted) as well as Potato and Pea Curry. You could also serve it with rice.

SERVES 4–6

5 tablespoons olive or canola oil
1 stick cinnamon
2 bay leaves
8 cardamom pods
$1\frac{1}{2}$ cups finely chopped onions
2 large cloves garlic, crushed to a pulp
One $1\frac{1}{2}$-inch piece fresh ginger, peeled and finely grated

2 pounds boneless lamb from the shoulder, cut into $1\frac{1}{4}$-inch pieces
$\frac{1}{2}$ teaspoon cayenne pepper
$1\frac{1}{4}$–$1\frac{1}{2}$ teaspoons salt
1 teaspoon homemade or store-bought *garam masala* (page 285)
4 tablespoons finely chopped fresh cilantro

Pour the oil into a wide, heavy pan and set over medium-high heat. When hot, put in the cinnamon, bay leaves, and cardamom. Let these sizzle for 10 seconds. Now add the onions. Stir and fry until the onion pieces start to turn brown at the edges. Add the garlic and ginger and stir once or twice. Now add the meat. Stir until it loses its raw color. Add the cayenne, salt, and $1\frac{1}{4}$ cups water. Stir and bring to a boil. Cover tightly, turn heat to low, and cook for 60–70 minutes or until the meat is tender. Remove lid and turn heat to high. Stir and cook until most of the liquid has been absorbed and the meat has a brownish (*bhuna*) look. Add the *garam masala* and cilantro. Stir to mix and turn off the heat.

Kashmiri Lamb Dumpukht

Dumpukht is a style of cooking that was made very popular in India in the Moghul courts starting around the sixteenth century. Meat or rice dishes were semiprepared or, in the case of meats, they were thoroughly marinated, and then put in a pot with a lid that was sealed shut with dough. The pot was placed on lightly smoldering embers. Some embers were also placed on the top of the lid, thus forming a kind of slow-cooking oven. When the dough seal was cracked and the lid removed, the aroma of the spices left the guests oohing and aahing. This cooking style is still very popular in India, Pakistan, and Bangladesh.

This is a royal-style dish, rich with almonds and saffron, which are native to Kashmir, and yet it is quite light. The recipe may easily be doubled.

For a festive meal, also serve Eggplants in a North-South Sesame/Peanut Sauce, and a rice dish.

SERVES 3–4

1¼ pounds boneless lamb, preferably from the shoulder, cut into 1½-inch cubes

1 cup whole-milk yogurt (preferably the Greek or acidophilus variety), lightly beaten with a fork until smooth

1½ teaspoons *garam masala* (preferably homemade, page 285)

¾ teaspoon cayenne pepper

1½ teaspoons salt

10 cardamom pods

¼ teaspoon whole black peppercorns

½ teaspoon saffron threads, crumbled

2 bay leaves

1 tablespoon golden raisins

20 whole almonds, preferably skinned, but unskinned will do

Combine all ingredients except the almonds in a nonreactive bowl. Prick the meat with the tip of a knife so that the marinade can penetrate well. Mix thoroughly, cover, and refrigerate overnight or up to 24 hours.

Pour hot water to cover the almonds and leave to soak overnight or up to 24 hours.

Preheat oven to 325°F.

Lift the almonds out of their soaking liquid and peel them if they are with skin. Put the meat, its marinade, and the almonds into a stove- and ovenproof pan. Bring to a low simmer over medium-low heat, stirring all the time so the yogurt does not curdle. Turn off the heat. Cover pan first with foil, crimping it tightly, and then with its lid. Place in the oven for 60–75 minutes, testing at the earlier time to see if the meat is tender; if not, return to the oven for 15 minutes.

Lamb Curry with Whole Spices

This is a very popular dish in Delhi, where it is made with bone-in cubes of goat meat. I generally make it with lamb.

I like to serve this with Indian flatbreads. Store-bought pita bread or tortillas would be good too. A vegetable and a legume should be included at dinnertime.

SERVES 4–6

6 tablespoons olive or canola oil

8 cardamom pods

Two 2-inch cinnamon sticks

8 whole cloves

1 teaspoon whole cumin seeds

1 teaspoon whole fennel seeds

1 cup (4 ounces) finely chopped onions

2 pounds boneless lamb from the shoulder, cut into 1½-inch pieces

1¼ cups yogurt (whole-milk or low-fat), lightly beaten

2 tablespoons ground coriander

2 teaspoons finely grated peeled fresh ginger, or 1 teaspoon powdered ginger

½–¾ teaspoon cayenne pepper

1½ teaspoons salt, or to taste

Preheat oven to 350°F.

Pour the oil into a large, wide, ovenproof pan and set over medium-high heat. When hot, put in the cardamom, cinnamon, cloves, cumin, and fennel and stir once. Add the onions and fry until they have just begun to turn brown. Add the meat and all the remaining ingredients. Stir to mix and bring to a simmer. Cover, first with foil, crimping the edges, and then with the lid, and place in the oven. Bake for 1¼ hours or until the meat is just tender, stirring now and then. Uncover and bake another 15–20 minutes or until the meat is a bit more dried out and slightly browned. Stir now and then during this period.

Kerala Lamb Stew

Pronounced "eshtew" by the locals, this aromatic, soul-satisfying stew is a much-loved dish, often eaten by the Syrian Christians of the southwestern state of Kerala at Easter. It has all the spices that grow in the backyards of Kerala homes—cinnamon, cardamom, cloves, and peppercorns. It also has the Kerala staple, coconut milk.

While it is generally served with the rice pancakes known as *appams* ("*appam* and stew" being somewhat akin to "meatloaf and mashed potatoes" or "rice and beans" or "ham and eggs"), plain jasmine rice is just as good.

SERVES 4–6

¼ cup olive or canola oil

Two 3-inch cinnamon sticks

½ teaspoon whole black peppercorns

10 whole cloves

10 cardamom pods

1 large (8 ounces) red onion, chopped finely

20 or so fresh curry leaves or 10 basil leaves, torn up

2 teaspoons very finely grated peeled fresh ginger

2 pounds stewing lamb

1 pound boiling potatoes, peeled and diced into 1-inch cubes

4 medium carrots, peeled and cut crossways into 1½-inch segments

1¾ teaspoon salt

¼–½ teaspoon cayenne pepper

1¼ cups coconut milk from a well-shaken can

Pour the oil into a large, heavy pan and set over medium-high heat. When hot, put in the cinnamon sticks, peppercorns, cloves, and cardamom. Let the spices sizzle for a few seconds. Put in the onions and stir and fry until they turn light brown. Add the curry leaves and ginger, then stir for a minute. Add the lamb and stir it around for 3–4 minutes. Now pour in 4 cups of water and bring to a boil. Cover, turn heat to low, and simmer 30 minutes.

Add the potatoes, carrots, salt, and cayenne. Stir and bring to a boil. Cover, turn heat to low, and cook 40 minutes or until the meat is tender. Add the coconut milk and crush a few of the potato pieces against the sides of the pan to thicken the sauce. Stir and bring to a simmer before serving.

Green Lamb Curry

Here is a most delicious curry from western India that may also be made with chicken. It requires a lot of cilantro. Buy a big bunch, or two if they are skimpy, aiming at about 6½–7 ounces. Once you have trimmed the cilantro by cutting off the lower, non-leafy stems, and washed and chopped it, you should end up with about 3½ ounces or about 2 packed cups.

The recipe may easily be doubled.

This curry may be eaten with a rice dish or Indian flatbreads. Mushroom and Pea Curry could be served on the side.

SERVES 3–4

2 tablespoons lemon juice

2 packed cups (3½ ounces) chopped cilantro

One 1-inch piece fresh ginger, peeled and chopped

4 good-sized cloves garlic, chopped

3–4 fresh hot green chilies (such as bird's-eye), chopped

½ teaspoon ground turmeric

1½ teaspoons salt

3 tablespoons olive or canola oil

½ teaspoon whole fennel seeds

1 medium onion, chopped

1¼ pounds boneless lamb, preferably from the shoulder, cut into 1–1½-inch cubes

½ cup coconut milk from a well-shaken can

Put the lemon juice, ½ cup water, chopped cilantro, ginger, garlic, chilies, turmeric, and salt, in this order, into a blender. Blend thoroughly, scraping down the sides, if necessary, with a rubber spatula, until you have a fine paste.

Preheat oven to 325°F.

Pour the oil into an ovenproof pan and set over medium-high heat. When hot, put in the fennel seeds. Two seconds later, put in the onions. Stir and fry until the onions turn brown at the edges. Add the meat. Stir and fry on high heat 7–8 minutes or until the meat is lightly browned. Add the green sauce from the blender and bring to a simmer. Cover and place pan in the oven. Bake for 60–75 minutes, then test to see if the meat is tender; if not, return to the oven for 15 minutes. Take the pan out of the oven and add the coconut milk. Stir it in. Reheat gently just before serving.

Rajasthani Red Meat

When this dish is served in the Rajasthan desert region of India, its color, coming mainly from ground hot chilies, is a fiery red. I have moderated the heat by mixing cayenne pepper with more calming paprika. Use a fresh red paprika if you want the proper color.

This is generally served with Indian flatbreads, but rice would be fine too. A calming green, such as spinach or Swiss chard, could be served on the side. For more robust flavors, have one of the eggplant dishes with it.

SERVES 4–6

¼ cup olive or canola oil

Two 3-inch cinnamon sticks

6 whole cloves

10 cardamom pods

1 large (8 ounces) red onion, chopped finely

2 teaspoons very finely grated peeled fresh ginger

4 garlic cloves, crushed to a pulp

1 tablespoon ground coriander

2 pounds stewing lamb, preferably from the shoulder

1½ teaspoons salt, or to taste

½–1 teaspoon cayenne pepper

2 tablespoons bright red paprika

3 tablespoons chopped fresh cilantro

Pour the oil into a large, heavy pan and set over medium-high heat. When hot, put in the cinnamon sticks, cloves, and cardamom. Let the spices sizzle for a few seconds. Put in the onions. Stir and fry until they turn a reddish brown. Add the ginger, garlic, and coriander. Stir for a minute. Add the lamb, salt, cayenne, and paprika. Stir the lamb around for 3–4 minutes. Now add 4 cups water and bring to a boil. Cover, turn heat to low, and simmer about 70 minutes or until the meat is tender. Sprinkle the cilantro over the top when serving.

Lamb Korma in an Almond-Saffron Sauce

This recipe may be easily doubled.
I just love it with Tomato Pullao.

SERVES 3–4

¼ cup slivered blanched almonds

One 1-inch piece fresh ginger, peeled and chopped

2 good-sized cloves garlic, chopped

3 tablespoons olive or canola oil

One 2–3-inch cinnamon stick

8 cardamom pods

5 whole cloves

2 bay leaves

1¼ pounds boneless lamb, preferably from the shoulder, cut into 1–1½-inch cubes

¾ teaspoon cayenne pepper

1¼ teaspoons salt

½ teaspoon saffron threads, crumbled

½ cup heavy cream

Soak the almonds in ½ cup boiling water for 2 hours. Put the almonds, their soaking liquid, the ginger, and garlic into a blender and blend until smooth.

Pour the oil into a medium pan and set over medium-high heat. When hot, add the cinnamon, cardamom, cloves, and bay leaves and stir-fry them for 5 seconds. Put in half the meat and brown on all sides. Remove the meat with tongs and put in a bowl. Brown the remaining meat the same way. Now return the first batch of browned meat to the pan. Pour in the paste from the blender. Add the cayenne, salt, and saffron. Stir and bring to a simmer. Cover, turn heat to low, and simmer gently for 60–75 minutes or until the meat is tender. Add the cream and cook on medium-high heat for a few minutes so the sauce thickens.

Lamb Shanks Braised
with Cardamom and Onion

Lamb shanks make for some of the best braised meat. The bone and marrow enrich the sauce and the gelatinous nature of the meat nearest the bone gives it a silken texture. In India we braise shanks in dozens of ways.

Muslim families sometimes eat the shanks for breakfast with all manner of flatbreads and raw onion relishes. You could serve them with rice as well, such as the Yellow Basmati Rice with Sesame Seeds.

SERVES 4

4 medium lamb shanks, about
    3½ pounds in all
Salt
Freshly ground black pepper
1½ cups plain yogurt, preferably the
    acidophilus yogurt sold in health-
    food stores, or Greek yogurt
6 cloves garlic, chopped
One 3-inch piece fresh ginger, peeled
    and chopped

3 tablespoons ground coriander
2 teaspoons ground cumin
½ teaspoon cayenne pepper
¼ cup olive or canola oil
10 cardamom pods
½ teaspoon whole black peppercorns
Two 3-inch cinnamon sticks
½ teaspoon whole cloves
1 medium onion, cut into fine half
    rings

Pat the shanks dry. Sprinkle them all over with ½ teaspoon salt and lots of freshly ground pepper.

Preheat oven to 325°F.

Put ½ cup of the yogurt, the garlic, and ginger into a blender and blend until smooth. Now add the coriander, cumin, cayenne, 1½ teaspoons salt, and the remaining 1 cup yogurt. Blend to mix.

Pour the oil into a very wide ovenproof sauté pan or wide casserole dish, large enough to hold the shanks easily in one layer, and set over medium-high heat. When hot, put in the cardamom, peppercorns, cinnamon, cloves, and shanks. Brown the shanks on one side. Turn them over, dropping the onion slices in the spaces between them. Brown the second side as well as the onions, moving the onions around in the pan as you need to. When the second side has browned, add the paste from the blender and 1 cup water. Bring to a boil. Cover and place the pan in the oven. Bake for 3 hours, turning the shanks over every 30 minutes.

CLOCKWISE FROM TOP: *Cinnamom Sticks, Cardamon Pods, and Cloves*

Pakistani Goat Curry with Potatoes

Goat is now increasingly available: it is sold at *halal* butchers, at West Indian butchers, and at specialty butchers. What you need are some pieces of meat with bone and some without bone. Ideally, the pieces should come from different parts of the animal—some from the shoulder, some from the upper leg, some from the shank, and a few from the neck—and should be cut into 1½-inch cubes. Bone pieces could be larger. I always like to include at least one marrowbone. You can make the same dish with lamb from the shoulder with some bone. Good lamb generally takes about 50–80 minutes to cook, less time than goat.

At home, we always ate this everyday dish with *chapati*s. There was always a *dal,* such as My Everyday Moong Dal, a couple of vegetables, and some relishes and chutneys. You may, of course, serve a simple rice dish instead of the bread.

SERVES 4

4 tablespoons olive oil, canola oil, or *ghee*
Two 2-inch cinnamon sticks
8 cardamom pods
1 large red onion, cut into very fine half rings
3 cloves garlic, crushed
1 tablespoon very finely chopped peeled fresh ginger
3 pounds goat meat for curries; see above

¼ teaspoon ground turmeric
1 tablespoon ground coriander
¼–½ teaspoon cayenne pepper
6 egg-sized potatoes, about 1 pound total, peeled and left whole
2 teaspoons salt
1 teaspoon *garam masala* (preferably the homemade kind, page 285)

Pour the oil into a large, wide, heavy pan and set over medium-high heat. When hot, put in the cinnamon, cardamom, and onions. Stir and fry 5–6 minutes or until the onions turn a light brown. Add the garlic and ginger. Stir for a minute. Add the goat, turmeric, coriander, and cayenne. Stir for 2–3 minutes. Add 1 cup water and bring to a boil. Cover and cook on medium heat about 10 minutes or until all the liquid has disappeared. Remove cover and stir 3–4 minutes to brown the meat slightly. Now add 4 cups water and bring to a boil. Cover, turn heat to low, and cook gently for 1 hour. Add the potatoes and salt. Stir and bring to a boil. Cover, turn heat to low, and cook gently for another 30 minutes or until the meat is very tender. Sprinkle the *garam masala* over the top and mix in. Turn off the heat and serve.

Anglo-Indian Sausage Patties

An Anglo-Indian acquaintance in Calcutta once told me that when he went to buy his sausages from the family butcher, he always took along the spices he wanted as flavoring. He would hand these to the butcher and then watch as his choice of meat was ground, seasoned, and pushed into casings. I made a note of the seasonings and now make those sausages all the time. I do not always bother with the casings. I make sausage patties, using all the same spices.

We eat these with eggs on Sundays, ensconced between slices of bread as sandwiches, or I put them into a curry (see next recipe), just as Anglo-Indian families have been doing over the years.

MAKES 8 PATTIES

1 pound ground pork (it is good if it is a bit fatty)

3 tablespoons finely chopped shallots or red onions

1 cup finely chopped cilantro

½–¾ teaspoon cayenne pepper

1 teaspoon *garam masala* (preferably homemade, page 285)

1 teaspoon salt

Lots of freshly ground black pepper

2 teaspoons oil

Put the pork in a bowl. Add the shallots, cilantro, cayenne, *garam masala,* salt, and pepper. Mix thoroughly, making sure to pick up and integrate all the shallot and cilantro bits. Make a loaf, wrap in plastic, and refrigerate overnight ideally or as little as 1–2 hours if you are rushed. Divide into 8 parts and form 8 smooth patties about 3 inches in diameter.

Pour the oil into a nonstick frying pan and set over medium-high heat. Put in the patties, as many as will fit in easily, and brown on both sides. This will take 4–5 minutes. Make sure that they are cooked through. Cook all patties this way. Remove with a slotted spatula.

Anglo-Indian Sausage Curry

You need the patties from the preceding recipe and the same pan used for browning them with its leftover oil. This is in fact a continuation of the last recipe and makes for a quick curry, good with rice, bread, and also with fried eggs and toast! So, make the preceding recipe, remove the patties from the frying pan with a slotted spatula, put them on a plate, and proceed immediately to make the curry sauce.

For a simple meal, serve with a rice dish and Corn with Aromatic Seasonings.

SERVES 3–4

2 tablespoons olive or canola oil
1 medium onion, finely chopped
1 teaspoon finely grated peeled fresh
    ginger
2 cloves garlic, crushed to a pulp
4 medium tomatoes, grated coarsely
    (page 289), or peeled and then
    finely chopped

$\frac{1}{2}$ teaspoon ground turmeric
$\frac{1}{2}$ teaspoon salt, or to taste
Lots of freshly ground black pepper
4–5 fresh hot green chilies (such as
    bird's-eye), slit halfway up, starting
    at the bottom end

Pour the oil into the same pan in which the sausage patties were fried and set on medium-high heat. When hot, put in the onions. Stir and fry the onions until they are lightly browned. Add the ginger and garlic. Stir for a minute. Put in the tomatoes and turmeric. Stir and cook on medium-high heat for 3 minutes or until the sauce has thickened and caramelized a bit. Now add 1 cup water and the salt, pepper, and green chilies. Stir and bring to a simmer. Cover, turn heat to low, and simmer gently for 5 minutes. Put the sausage patties back into the pan, in a single layer if possible, spoon the sauce over them, cover, and heat them through.

Hot, Salty, and Sweet Pork Chops

Chinese influence in India is ancient—the two nations have been trading since the BCs. The older Chinese restaurants in the major cities serve an Indianized version of Chinese food, and Indians at home think nothing of adding a bit of soy sauce to this and that. Here is one such modern dish. Ideally, the pork should be marinated overnight.

Plain Jasmine Rice and any vegetable dish would be perfect.

SERVES 4

FOR THE MARINADE
¼ teaspoon salt
½ tablespoon whole coriander seeds
2 teaspoons whole cumin seeds
One 2-inch cinnamon stick
1 teaspoon whole fennel seeds
1 teaspoon whole peppercorns
½ teaspoon cayenne pepper

YOU ALSO NEED
2 pounds thin (⅓-inch-thick) center-cut pork chops (4 chops)
3 tablespoons olive or canola oil
½ medium onion, chopped
1 teaspoon finely grated peeled fresh ginger
3 tablespoons soy sauce
1½ tablespoons sugar

Put all the ingredients for the marinade in a clean coffee grinder or other spice grinder and grind as finely as possible. Sprinkle spices evenly on both sides of the pork chops and pat them in. Cover the chops and refrigerate at least 6 hours or overnight. (Twenty-four hours would be fine too.)

Pour the oil into a large frying pan and set over medium-high heat. When hot, put in the pork chops, and brown on both sides. Remove to a bowl. Put in the onions, lowering heat a bit, and brown them. Add the ginger and stir once. Now put in the pork chops in a single layer and add the soy sauce, sugar, and 1 cup water. Bring to a boil. Cover, turn heat to low, and simmer gently for 50 minutes or until chops are tender, turning the chops every 10 minutes. Reduce sauce until it is syrupy and clings to the chops.

Pork (or Lamb) with Lentils

Indians love dried beans and split peas, eating them in some form at every single meal. They are sometimes cooked on their own, but they can also be combined with vegetables, fish, or meat. This recipe is for pork and lentils, but you could use lamb, if you prefer it. Ideally, make this dish ahead of time, as the lentils absorb a lot of liquid after the cooking is done.

Served with a salad and relishes, this becomes a meal in itself.

SERVES 4

2 teaspoons ground cumin seeds
4 teaspoons ground coriander seeds
½ teaspoon ground turmeric
½ teaspoon cayenne pepper
3 tablespoons olive or canola oil
¼ cup finely chopped onions
1 teaspoon finely grated peeled fresh ginger

1½ cups (8 ounces) finely chopped tomatoes
1½ pounds boneless pork from the shoulder, cut into 1½-inch cubes
1 cup green lentils, washed and drained
1½ teaspoons salt, or to taste

Toss the cumin, coriander, turmeric, and cayenne together in a small bowl. Add 2 tablespoons water. Stir to mix.

Pour the oil into a large, wide pan and set over medium heat. When hot, put in the onions. Stir and sauté about 3 minutes, until the onion pieces turn brown at the edges. Add the ginger and cook and stir for half a minute. Add the spice paste and stir for a minute. Add the tomatoes. Stir and cook them for 2–3 minutes. Add the meat. Stir and cook it for 2–3 minutes. Pour in 1 cup water and bring to a boil. Cover and cook on medium-high heat for 10 minutes, stirring from the bottom now and then. When the sauce is greatly reduced, add the lentils, 3½ cups water, and salt. Stir and bring to a simmer. Cover partially and cook for 40 minutes or until lentils are tender. Check for salt, adding more if needed.

Calf's Liver with Onions

Here I have taken a Pakistani recipe for stir-fried liver made in the wok-like *karhai* and changed it just enough so Westerners, who like their liver softer and pinker than South Asians do, may enjoy it too. If you want the Pakistani recipe, after the liver has browned, cut it crossways into 1-inch squares and add these pieces to the onion sauce when it is ready. Continue to stir and cook on low heat until the liver is done to your satisfaction.

Serve with rice and a salad or a green vegetable.

SERVES 2

2 slices of calf's liver, about ¾ pound in all
Salt
¼ teaspoon ground turmeric
Cayenne pepper
3 tablespoons olive or canola oil
¼ teaspoon whole cumin seeds
1 good-sized onion (about 7–8 ounces), cut into ¼-inch half rings

1 clove garlic, crushed to a pulp
½ teaspoon ground mustard (the commonly available yellow powder)
1 medium tomato, grated (page 289)
1 fresh hot green chili (such as bird's-eye), chopped finely (optional)
Freshly ground black pepper
1–2 teaspoons lemon juice

Lay the liver slices down flat and rub ¼ teaspoon salt, the turmeric, and ⅛ teaspoon cayenne pepper on both sides. Cover and set aside for 30 minutes. (All the other ingredients may be prepared at this time.)

Pour 1 tablespoon of the oil into a nonstick frying pan and set on medium-high heat. When hot, put in the liver slices. Cook the first side until browned, about 1½–2 minutes. Turn the slices over and cook the second side the same way. If you want the slices a bit more done, lower heat to medium and cook both sides 30–60 seconds more. Remove to a serving dish and keep warm.

Add the remaining 2 tablespoons oil to the frying pan, still set over medium-high heat. When hot, put in the cumin seeds. Ten seconds later, put in the onions. Stir a few times and lower heat to medium. Stir and fry the onions 6–8 minutes or until they have softened a bit and browned slightly on the edges. Add the garlic and stir a few times. Now put in the mustard, tomato, green chili, black pepper, lemon juice, and ¼–⅓ teaspoon salt. Stir and cook for a minute. Pour this sauce on top of the liver slices and serve.

Beef or Lamb Jhal Faraizi

This dish is a specialty of the mixed-race Anglo-Indian community and probably started out as a way to use up leftover roasts of lamb or beef. When there were no leftovers and there was a craving for the dish, fresh meat was diced into small pieces and boiled with a little salt and ginger until it was tender, and this was used instead. These days you can buy roast beef from a delicatessen (ask them to cut ⅓-inch slices—you will just need a few) and use those, or make use of leftover meats.

There are many versions of the *jhal faraizi*, most being stir-fries of julienned meat, onions, and both hot and sweet peppers. *Jhal* means heat from hot chilies, so chilies are an essential ingredient, either in their fresh green form or their dried red form. I found the version below in an old, thin Anglo-Indian cookery book in Calcutta, and this is the version I like best. It is like a hash, only it is spicy!

You may serve this at breakfast with or without eggs or by itself with a salad.

SERVES 2–4

¾ pound boiling potatoes
2 tablespoons olive or canola oil
½ teaspoon whole cumin seeds
1 medium onion, cut into ⅓-inch dice
2–3 fresh hot green chilies (such as
  bird's-eye), chopped

¾ pound roasted beef or lamb, diced
1 teaspoon salt
Freshly ground black pepper

Boil the potatoes ahead of time and then leave them to cool. Peel them and then cut them into ⅓-inch dice.

Pour the oil into a large, preferably nonstick frying pan and set over medium-high heat. When hot, put in the cumin seeds. Let them sizzle for 5 seconds. Add the onions, potatoes, and green chilies. Turn heat to medium.

Stir and fry for about 5 minutes or until the onions turn somewhat translucent. Now add the meat, salt, and lots of black pepper. Stir and mix for a minute. Turn the heat down slightly so it is on medium low. Press down on all the ingredients in the pan with a spatula to form a flat cake that covers the entire bottom. Let the bottom brown for about 15 minutes. You can shift and turn the pan slightly so that all of the bottom browns evenly. Break up the cake and serve hot.

Baked Beef Curry

Beef is eaten by Muslims throughout India, Pakistan, and Bangladesh and is often referred to as *bara gosht,* or "big meat." It is sometimes "baked" using an ancient top-of-the-stove method known as *dum.* A tightly closed pot with the meat inside (or it could be rice and meat) is placed over low embers and more charcoal is placed on top of the flat lid. With heat coming from the top and the bottom, a slow baking ensues. When the pot is opened, the aromas permeate the room to great cries of appreciation. I find that an oven can, very conveniently, do a *dum* with similar results.

Serve with rice or Indian breads. Black Beans are also good on the side along with vegetables and relishes for an elegant meal.

SERVES 4–6

6 tablespoons olive or canola oil

6 cardamom pods

Two 2-inch cinnamon sticks

2 pounds stewing beef, cut into
    1½-inch pieces

1 teaspoon whole cumin seeds

2 cups (8 ounces) chopped onions

1¼ cups yogurt (whole-milk or low-fat), lightly beaten

2 tablespoons ground coriander

2 teaspoons finely grated peeled fresh
    ginger, or 1 teaspoon powdered
    ginger

¼–½ teaspoon cayenne pepper

1½ teaspoons salt, or to taste

Preheat oven to 350°F.

Pour the oil into a large, wide, ovenproof pan and set over medium-high heat. When hot, put in the cardamom and cinnamon. Stir once, and put in only as much of the meat as will brown easily. Brown on all sides and remove to a bowl with a slotted spoon. Brown the remaining meat this way. Add the cumin seeds and onions to the oil in the pan and fry until the onion pieces have just begun to turn brown. Turn off the heat.

Return the meat and all accumulated juices to the pan as well as all the remaining ingredients. Stir to mix, and bring to a simmer. Cover, first with foil, crimping the edges, and then with the lid, and place in the oven. Bake for 1½ hours or until the meat is tender.

Sri Lankan Beef Smore

This is a pot roast. It is a specialty of Sri Lanka's Burgher community, which owes its origins to a happy mixture of European colonialists, mostly Dutch but some Portuguese and English as well, with the local population. Burgher cuisine is a glorious by-product of this union. Here, a simple pot roast has been made wonderfully Sri Lankan with the addition of roasted coriander, cumin, and fennel seeds—the main ingredients in Sri Lankan curry powders—and, of course, coconut milk. Some people add a little simple lime pickle, or tamarind water or vinegar, to give it a tart edge. I have used red wine vinegar.

A few simple steps are required here: The spices need to be roasted and ground. Then, after the meat is browned, everything goes into a pot and is braised slowly in the oven.

The meat is sliced, and some of its own sauce is ladled over the top. It may then be served with rice, noodles (Sri Lanka has exquisite rice noodles, so Thin Rice Noodles would work), or mashed potatoes, if you prefer.

SERVES 4–6

One 2½-pound piece of beef (shoulder meat, tied as a roast, or a piece of chuck, or even brisket—any beef chunk suitable for braising)
Salt
Freshly ground black pepper
4 teaspoons whole coriander seeds
1 teaspoon whole cumin seeds
1 teaspoon whole fennel seeds
¼ teaspoon whole fenugreek seeds
4 tablespoons olive or canola oil

One 2-inch cinnamon stick
1 large onion, finely chopped
One 2-inch piece fresh ginger, peeled and finely grated
4 cloves garlic, finely chopped
2 tablespoons red wine vinegar
1½ cups beef or chicken stock
½–1 teaspoon cayenne pepper
1 cup coconut milk from a well-shaken can

Pat the meat dry and sprinkle lightly with salt and lots of black pepper.

Set a small cast-iron or other heavy frying pan over medium heat. When very hot, sprinkle in the coriander, cumin, fennel, and fenugreek seeds. Stir for 30 seconds or so until the spices just start to emit a roasted aroma. Empty onto a piece of paper towel, and, when cooled off a bit, grind the spices in a clean coffee grinder or crush in a mortar.

Preheat oven to 325°F.

Pour the oil into an ovenproof casserole-type pan and set over medium-high heat. When hot, put in the meat and brown on all sides. Remove to a plate. Add the cinnamon, onions, ginger, and garlic. Stir and cook 4–5 minutes. Add the vinegar, stock, cayenne, $1\frac{1}{2}$ teaspoons salt, and the beef as well as its accumulated juices. Bring to a boil, stirring the sauce. Cover and place in oven. Cook, basting and turning every 20 minutes or so, about 2–$2\frac{1}{2}$ hours or until meat is tender. Remove pan from oven. Add the coconut milk, stir, and bring to a simmer before serving.

Vegetables

India has some of the best-tasting vegetables in the world, all available fresh, daily, at very reasonable prices. Indian tomatoes—and here I include those found in Pakistan, Sri Lanka, and Bangladesh—may look squiggly and misshapen, but they have better texture and flavor than what I find much of the year in Britain and the United States. The same holds true for cabbage, cauliflower, and almost any other vegetable that you can name. South Asia eats many more types of vegetables too. From snake gourds to wing beans, green plantains to green jackfruit, the best vegetables from around the world have found their way here, and each is cooked in hundreds of different ways.

Green beans may be cooked very simply with mustard, cumin, and sesame seeds; winter carrots are often just sliced and stir-fried with fresh fenugreek greens or, failing that, with cilantro; monsoon corn either is just roasted, like chestnuts, or its grains are stir-fried with green chilies, ginger, cinnamon, and cardamom. Then there is eggplant, the very popular "meaty" vegetable that is thought to have originated in India. It is fried into fritters, partially quartered and stuffed, combined with dumplings, made into pilafs, stewed with tomatoes, cooked with quinces, roasted and put into yogurt *raitas*—I could do a whole book of South Asian eggplant recipes!

And I could do the same with potatoes. Even though potatoes came to India from the West, the nation took to them like ducks to water. One wit in Calcutta is known to have remarked that the only good thing the British ever gave to India was the potato. Its starchy texture lent itself beautifully to South Asia's array of spices: it was stewed with tomatoes and ginger, stir-fried with asafetida and cumin, combined with peas and cauliflower, and made into curries flavored with chilies and mustard seeds.

For this chapter, I have selected more than two dozen of the simpler recipes, all for vegetables that can be found easily in the West. They will provide endless variety to vegetarian diets. Meat and fish eaters will be able to spice up entire meals with new aromas, textures, and tastes. And here is another thing. You should not feel obliged to make a complete Indian meal every time you want to cook one of these vegetable dishes. Try an Indian potato dish with broiled chicken instead of boiled potatoes; have an Indian corn dish with frankfurters or sausages. Enjoy mixing and matching— anything to make your life easier and your meals more exciting.

South Indian–Style Green Beans

South Indian vegetables can be very simply prepared. Here green beans are blanched and then quickly stir-fried with spices.

These can be served with any meat, poultry, or fish dish, South Asian or Western.

Salt

1 pound green beans, trimmed and cut into 1-inch lengths

3 tablespoons olive or canola oil

$\frac{1}{2}$ teaspoon whole cumin seeds

$\frac{1}{2}$ teaspoon whole brown or yellow mustard seeds

$\frac{1}{2}$ teaspoon sesame seeds

$\frac{1}{8}$ teaspoon cayenne pepper

Bring 8 cups water to a boil. Add 1 tablespoon salt to it and then the cut beans. Boil for 4–5 minutes or until the beans are just tender. Drain immediately and leave in the colander.

Pour the oil into a frying pan and set over medium-high heat. When hot, put in the cumin, mustard, and sesame seeds. As soon as the seeds start popping, a matter of seconds, take the pan off the heat and stir in the beans. Put the pan back on the stove, turning the heat down to medium low. Stir to mix for about a minute, adding $\frac{1}{2}$ teaspoon salt and the cayenne. Remove pan from heat.

Karhai Broccoli

This is a stir-fried broccoli dish.

A *karhai* is the Indian wok that actually predated the Chinese wok and has been used since ancient times for deep-frying, for reducing milk for dozens of Indian desserts, and for stir-frying and sautéing.

Broccoli, once unknown in India, is now found in many specialty markets. For this recipe I use a nice-sized bunch (about 2 pounds) and use most of the stems as well, after peeling them and cutting them crossways into thickish slices. I cut the broccoli head into small florets, each no longer than $1\frac{1}{2}$ inches— with each small head attached to a bit of stem so it retains its elegance.

Serve at Indian or Western meals.

SERVES 4

3 tablespoons olive or canola oil
$\frac{1}{8}$ teaspoon ground asafetida
$\frac{1}{4}$ teaspoon whole cumin seeds
$\frac{1}{4}$ teaspoon whole mustard seeds

6 cups trimmed and cut broccoli (see instruction above)
$\frac{1}{2}$ teaspoon salt
$\frac{1}{4}$ teaspoon cayenne pepper

Pour the oil into a wok or medium frying pan and set over medium-high heat. When hot, put in the asafetida and then the cumin and mustard seeds. As soon as the mustard seeds begin to pop, a matter of seconds, toss in the broccoli. Stir and fry for a minute, adding the salt and cayenne as you do so. Pour in $\frac{1}{4}$ cup water and bring to a simmer. Cover, turn heat to low, and cook 7–8 minutes or until broccoli is just tender, stirring now and then.

Carrots with Cilantro

Here is an everyday carrot dish.

In India it is served hot, but I often serve it cold in the summer, almost like a carrot salad.

SERVES 4

2 tablespoons peanut or olive oil

$\frac{1}{8}$ teaspoon ground asafetida

$\frac{1}{4}$ teaspoon whole cumin seeds

1 pound carrots, peeled and cut into $\frac{1}{3}$-inch-thick rounds

1 well-packed cup very finely chopped cilantro

$\frac{1}{2}$ teaspoon salt

$\frac{1}{8}$–$\frac{1}{4}$ teaspoon cayenne pepper

Pour the oil into a medium frying pan and set over medium-high heat. When hot, put in the asafetida and cumin. Stir once or twice and toss in the carrots. Stir once and turn off the heat. Add all the remaining ingredients and 3 tablespoons water. Stir well and bring to a simmer over medium heat. Cover, turn heat to very low, and simmer very gently for 3–4 minutes or until carrots are done, stirring once or twice during this period.

Swiss Chard with Ginger and Garlic

In North India, greens are often cooked simply, with ginger, garlic, and chili powder or green chilies.

Indians love eating greens at all meals. They go well with meats. If you are having a simple Indian meal of *dal* and rice, all you need to add is a green and a relish, perhaps with yogurt in it.

SERVES 4

1½ pounds Swiss chard, well washed
3 tablespoons olive or canola oil
1 clove garlic, cut into long slivers

1 teaspoon slivered peeled fresh ginger
½ teaspoon salt
¼ teaspoon cayenne pepper

Hold several chard leaves together and, starting at the stem end, cut the stems and leaves crossways, at ¼-inch intervals.

Pour the oil into a large pot and place on medium-high heat. When hot, put in the garlic and ginger. Stir a few times. Put in all the chard, with some of the washing water still clinging to the leaves. Cover. As soon as the leaves have wilted, a matter of a few minutes, add the salt and cayenne. Stir to mix. Cover again and turn heat to low. Cook 5 minutes or until chard is just done.

Corn with Aromatic Seasonings

This is an easy, perfumed, stir-fried corn dish that can be made with fresh or frozen corn.

This may be served with most Indian meals but also goes well with Western-style roasted or grilled pork, duck, and chicken.

3 tablespoons olive or canola oil
1 teaspoon whole brown or yellow
    mustard seeds
4 cardamom pods
4 whole cloves
One 1-inch cinnamon stick
2 bay leaves
1 teaspoon finely grated peeled fresh
    ginger

1–2 teaspoons finely chopped fresh hot
    green chilies (do not discard seeds)
4 cups corn cut fresh off the cobs, or
    two 10-ounce packets of frozen
    corn, defrosted and drained
1 teaspoon salt
¼ cup heavy cream

Pour the oil into a frying pan and set over medium heat. Meanwhile, combine the mustard seeds, cardamom, cloves, cinnamon, and bay leaves in a small cup. When the oil is hot, put in all the whole spices. As soon as the mustard seeds pop, a matter of seconds, put in the ginger and green chilies. Stir once or twice and then add in the corn. Stir for 2–3 minutes. Add the salt and cream. Continue to stir and cook for another minute. Turn heat to low and cook 1–2 minutes, stirring, until all the cream is absorbed.

You can pick out and discard the cardamom pods, cloves, cinnamon, and bay leaves if you are serving those unaccustomed to large whole spices in their foods.

Eggplant with Tomatoes

You need medium-sized egglants for this. I use the purple kind, 5 of them, each weighing about 5 ounces, and then cut them, unskinned, into 2"×1" chunks, each chunk with skin on at least one side. Normally, eggplant chunks require frying first to give them their unctuous, satiny texture, after which they may be folded into a variety of sauces—here it is a tomato sauce. But I have found a less oily way around that; I broil them instead.

You serve this dish hot with a lamb or chicken curry or cold, as a salad, with cold meats, Indian (such as Tandoori-Style Chicken with Mint) or Western.

SERVES 4–6

1½–1¾ pounds medium-sized eggplants, cut into chunks as suggested above
Salt
5 tablespoons olive, canola, or peanut oil
1 teaspoon whole black or yellow mustard seeds
½ teaspoon whole cumin seeds

½ teaspoon whole fennel seeds
½ teaspoon whole nigella seeds (if available)
1 dried hot red chili
2 cloves garlic, chopped
2 cups (12 ounces) peeled and chopped tomatoes, or grated tomatoes (page 289)
¼ teaspoon sugar

Turn on the broiler, arranging a shelf so it is 5–6 inches from the source of the heat. Spread the eggplant chunks in a baking tray. Sprinkle them with ½ teaspoon salt and 2 tablespoons of the oil. Toss and put under the broiler. Broil for about 15 minutes, tossing now and then, until all sides are lightly browned.

Pour the remaining 3 tablespoons oil into a large sauté pan and set over medium-high heat. When hot, put in the mustard seeds, cumin seeds, fennel seeds, nigella, and chili. As soon as the mustard seeds begin to pop, a matter of seconds, toss in the garlic. Stir a few times, until the garlic is golden, and then quickly put in the tomatoes, eggplants, ¼ teaspoon salt, and the sugar. Mix and bring to a simmer. Cover, turn heat to low, and simmer gently about 20 minutes, stirring now and then, until the eggplants are tender and smothered in the sauce.

Sweet-and-Sour Eggplant

Eggplants come in so many sizes and shapes. You may use 4 of the purple "baby" Italian eggplants (aim for 1¼ pounds), 4 Japanese eggplants, or 8 of the very small Indian ones. All are quartered partially—the top, sepal end always stays attached so the eggplants retain their shape—and then stuffed with a spice mixture before being cooked. For the mixture to hold, a little starch needs to be added. In India, this is the very nutritious chickpea flour. You may use cornmeal or masa harina instead if you have them at hand. All will need to be slightly roasted first. This is easily done in a small cast-iron frying pan.

This very gratifying dish may be served as a main course, along with a green vegetable, some *dal* (such as Black Beans), rice, and a yogurt relish. It would also go well with hearty chicken and lamb curries.

SERVES 4

4 (about 1¼ pounds total) purple baby eggplants, or see above

2 tablespoons chickpea flour

1 teaspoon very finely grated peeled fresh ginger

¼–½ teaspoon cayenne pepper

1½ tablespoons ground coriander

1 teaspoon ground cumin

Salt

3 tablespoons finely chopped cilantro

4 tablespoons olive or canola oil

2 teaspoons sugar

2 teaspoons lemon juice

Cut the eggplants in quarters lengthways, without separating the pieces at the stem end. Leave to soak in a bowl of water for 30 minutes.

Put the chickpea flour in a small cast-iron frying pan. Stir on medium heat until it is a shade darker. Remove to a small bowl. Add the ginger, cayenne, coriander, cumin, ¾ teaspoon salt, cilantro, and ¼ cup water. Stir to make a paste.

Remove eggplants from the soaking water and dry them off. Rub the spice mixture on all the cut surfaces. Pour the oil into a medium frying pan and set on medium-high heat. When hot, put in the eggplants and brown them lightly on all sides. Sprinkle ¼ teaspoon salt over the top and add ¼ cup water. Bring to a simmer. Cover, turn heat to low, and cook gently for 25 minutes or until tender.

Meanwhile, combine ¼ cup water with the sugar and lemon juice. Pour this over the eggplants when they are tender. Cook on medium-high heat, turning the eggplants gently once, until only a thick sauce remains.

Eggplants in a North-South Sauce

This is one of our most beloved family dishes. It is very much in the Hyderabadi style, where North Indian and South Indian seasonings are combined. Over the years, I have simplified the recipe. Here, you may use the long, tender Japanese eggplants or the purple "baby" Italian eggplants or even the striated purple and white ones that are about the same size as the baby Italian ones. Once cut, what you are aiming for are 1-inch chunks with as much skin on them as possible so they do not fall apart.

Serve this hot with meat or vegetable curries, rice, and *dal* or serve it cold, as a salad, with cold meats, Indian (see Chicken Karhai with Mint) or Western. I love it with slices of ham.

SERVES 4–6

4 tablespoons olive or canola oil
$\frac{1}{8}$ teaspoon ground asafetida
$\frac{1}{2}$ teaspoon skinned *urad dal* or yellow split peas
$\frac{1}{2}$ teaspoon whole mustard seeds
$\frac{1}{2}$ teaspoon whole cumin seeds
$\frac{1}{2}$ teaspoon whole nigella seeds (*kalonji*)
$\frac{1}{2}$ teaspoon whole fennel seeds
1 medium onion, chopped
2 cloves garlic, chopped

$1\frac{1}{2}$ pounds slim Japanese eggplants, cut crossways into 1-inch segments, or "baby" Italian eggplants cut in half lengthways and then crossways, into 1-inch segments
2 medium tomatoes, grated (see page 289), about $1\frac{1}{4}$ cups
1 cup chicken stock or water
1 teaspoon salt
$\frac{1}{4}$–$\frac{1}{2}$ teaspoon cayenne pepper

Pour the oil into a very large frying pan and set over medium-high heat. When hot, put in the asafetida and the *urad dal*. As soon as the *dal* turns a shade darker, add the mustard, cumin, nigella, and fennel seeds, in that order. When the mustard seeds begin to pop, a matter of seconds, add the onions. Stir and fry for a minute. Add the garlic and the eggplant. Stir and fry for 4–5 minutes or until the onions are a bit browned. Add the grated tomatoes, stock, salt, and cayenne. Stir to mix and bring to a boil. Cover, turn heat to low, and cook about 20 minutes or until the eggplants are tender, stirring now and then.

TOP: *Sweet-and-Sour Butternut Squash*
LEFT: *Mushroom and Pea Curry*
BOTTOM: *Eggplants in a North-South Sauce*

Eggplants in a North-South Sesame/Peanut Sauce

This is a richer, nuttier variation on the last recipe.

SERVES 4–6

Follow the preceding recipe. Ten minutes before the cooking time is up, put 2 tablespoons sesame paste or peanut butter in a small bowl. Slowly add ½ cup of chicken stock or water and mix well. Add this mixture to the pan and stir it in. Cover and continue cooking gently until the eggplants are tender.

Kashmiri-Style Collard Greens

One of my cousins was married to a Kashmiri gentleman, and for the period when he was working at the United Nations in New York he had brought along a manservant. My cousin let me have him once a week to cook and clean. His repertoire was limited—he could only cook dishes he had learned from my cousin, such as this simple Kashmiri staple, which we loved. Soon he was making it week after week, and it remains one of our favorites. In Kashmir, collard-type greens and rice are eaten as commonly as beans and rice in Central America, the season for them lasting from spring (when the greens are tender) until the snows start to fall in early winter (when the greens get coarser).

Note: Young greens will cook faster. So if you are using them, start with half the stock and add more if needed.

Serve with rice and either a *dal* or a meat curry.

SERVES 6

1¾ pounds collard greens
3 tablespoons olive or canola oil
⅛ teaspoon ground asafetida

3 dried hot red chilies (the short cayenne type)
2 cups chicken stock or water
Salt

Wash the collard greens and then remove their stems and coarse central veins. Stack 6–7 leaves on top of each other and roll them up lengthways. Cut crossways to get ½-inch ribbons. Now cut lengthways to get ½-inch pieces.

Pour the oil into a large pot and set over medium-high heat. When hot, put in the asafetida and the chilies. As soon as the chilies darken, a matter of seconds, take the pan off the heat briefly to add the greens and the stock. Put the pan back on the heat and bring to a boil. Cover, turn heat to medium low, and cook 30–40 minutes or until greens are tender. Remove cover and taste. Seasoned stock may require only ½ teaspoon salt. Add what is needed. Turn the heat to medium high and boil away most of the liquid. If you are eating the greens with rice, you may want to save some extra juice to moisten it adequately.

Mushroom Bhaaji

For this dish of stir-fried mushrooms, I use largish white mushrooms, but if your mushrooms are medium-sized, you should just halve them.

Serve this as a part of an Indian meal, along with rice or breads, a fish dish, and a relish, or have it with scrambled eggs for brunch.

SERVES 3–4

3 tablespoons olive or canola oil
½ teaspoon whole brown mustard
   seeds
½ teaspoon whole cumin seeds
¼ cup finely chopped onions
10 ounces largish white mushrooms,
   quartered

1 clove garlic, crushed in a garlic press
3 tablespoons plain yogurt
⅛ teaspoon cayenne pepper
1 teaspoon ground coriander
½ teaspoon salt
2 tablespoons finely chopped cilantro

Pour the oil into a frying pan and set over medium heat. When hot, put in the mustard and cumin seeds. As soon as the mustard seeds start to pop, a matter of seconds, put in the onions. Stir and fry until onions start to turn brown at the edges. Put in the mushrooms and stir for a minute. Take the pan off the heat and put in the garlic, yogurt, cayenne, coriander, and salt. Put the pan back on medium heat and stir well. Keep cooking and stirring until all the yogurt is absorbed, a few minutes. Stir in the cilantro toward the end.

Mushroom and Pea Curry

I like to use cremini mushrooms, as they have a firmer texture, but if you cannot get them, ordinary, medium-sized white mushrooms will do. Remember that a relatively firm tomato can be peeled with a paring knife like an apple.

A great curry for vegetarians and meat eaters alike. Serve with rice or Indian bread and some relishes.

SERVES 4

1 tablespoon ground coriander

1½ teaspoons ground cumin

¼ teaspoon ground turmeric

¼ teaspoon cayenne pepper

3 tablespoons olive or canola oil

¼ cup (1¾ ounces) finely chopped onions

1 teaspoon finely grated peeled fresh ginger

1½ cups (7–8 ounces) peeled and finely chopped tomato, see above

1¼ teaspoons salt, or to taste

1 pound cremini mushrooms, halved lengthways

10 ounces green peas, fresh or frozen and defrosted

Combine the coriander, cumin, turmeric, and cayenne in a small bowl. Add about 1½ tablespoons water and mix to make a paste.

Pour the oil into a medium pan and set over medium heat. When hot, put in the onions. Stir and sauté for 3–4 minutes or until the pieces are brown at the edges. Add the ginger and stir 3–4 times. Add the spice paste. Stir and cook for about a minute. Add the tomato. Stir and cook, scraping up from the bottom, for about 4 minutes or until the tomato has softened. Add 2 cups water and the salt. Stir and bring to a boil. Cover, turn heat to low, and simmer 20 minutes.

Add the mushrooms and bring to a boil. Cover and cook on low heat for 10 minutes. Add the peas. Bring to a boil. Cover and cook on low heat for 5 minutes or until the peas are done. Check for salt, adding a bit more if needed.

Okra with Shallots (*Bhuni Bhindi*)

This is easily my favorite okra recipe, though I must admit to loving plain, crisply fried okra as well. Okra is a vastly misunderstood vegetable. First of all, it should be young and crisp when it is harvested. Then, it should be cooked so its mucilaginous quality (that is, its slimy aspect) is somewhat reduced. Look for small, tender okra. They are the best.

Pinkish-red onions in the north and shallots in the south are the onions of India. As shallots seem to be getting larger and larger, I suggest that you use about 3 of the larger ones here.

When I was a child, all I wanted for lunch was this okra dish, some *chapatis,* My Everyday Moong Dal, and a yogurt relish. You may, of course, serve this with meat curries as well.

SERVES 4

12 ounces fresh okra

¼ cup olive, canola, or peanut oil

½ teaspoon whole cumin seeds

¾ cup (2 ounces) shallots, or onions that have been peeled, cut in half lengthwise, and cut into fine half rings

1½ teaspoons ground coriander

¼ teaspoon crushed red chilies

½ teaspoon salt

1 teaspoon lemon juice

Cut off the top stem ends and the very tips of the okra pods. You can do 3–4 at the same time. Now cut each pod diagonally into 3–4 slices, depending upon size.

Pour the oil into a medium frying pan and set over medium-high heat. When hot, put in the cumin seeds. A few seconds later, put in all the sliced okra. Stir and fry for about 5 minutes. The okra will have browned a bit. Add the shallots and continue to stir and fry for about 3 minutes so that the shallots brown as well. Now turn the heat to low. Add the coriander, red chilies, and salt. Stir and keep cooking another 7–9 minutes or until the okra is crisp and cooked through. Add the lemon juice and stir to mix.

Gujarati-Style Okra

An everyday vegetable dish, this time in the Gujarati style of western India, made without onions. Because of its viscosity, okra is never washed. Instead, it is wiped with a damp cloth and left for a while to air-dry before it is cut.

This dish is generally eaten with legume dishes, other vegetables, yogurt relishes, pickles, and Indian breads.

SERVES 4

3 tablespoons olive or canola oil

A generous pinch of ground asafetida

$\frac{1}{2}$ teaspoon whole brown or yellow mustard seeds

1 pound fresh okra (pick small, tender pods), top and tail removed and then cut crossways at $\frac{1}{2}$-inch intervals

$\frac{1}{8}$ teaspoon ground turmeric

1 teaspoon salt

$\frac{1}{2}$ teaspoon ground cumin

$\frac{1}{2}$ teaspoon ground coriander

$\frac{1}{4}$–$\frac{1}{2}$ teaspoon cayenne pepper, or to taste

Pour the oil into a frying pan and set over medium-high heat. When hot, put in the asafetida and mustard seeds. As soon as the mustard seeds begin to pop, a matter of seconds, add the okra. Turn heat to medium. Stir and cook for 3 minutes. Add the turmeric and salt and toss well. Turn heat to medium low. Stir and cook for 8–9 minutes or until the okra is lightly browned and almost cooked. Sprinkle in the cumin, coriander, and cayenne. Toss, turn heat to low, and cook another 2 minutes.

Potatoes with Cumin and Mustard Seeds

We eat these potatoes with our eggs on Sundays, with our Indian meals, and also with our more Western roasts and grills. They are versatile and good.

SERVES 3–4

1½ pounds waxy boiling potatoes, boiled until just done, cooled thoroughly, and peeled
¼ cup olive or canola oil
½ teaspoon whole cumin seeds
½ teaspoon whole brown or yellow mustard seeds

1 teaspoon finely slivered peeled fresh ginger (see box below)
½ teaspoon salt, or to taste
¼ teaspoon crushed red pepper flakes, or more, if desired
Freshly ground black pepper

Cut the potatoes into ½"×⅓" dice.

Pour the oil into a frying pan and set over medium-high heat. When hot, put in the cumin and mustard seeds. As soon as the mustard seeds begin to pop, a matter of seconds, put in the ginger. Stir twice and add the potatoes. Sprinkle the salt, red pepper, and black pepper over the top. Now stir and fry for 4–5 minutes. The potatoes should get lightly browned, and all the spices should be well mixed. Taste for salt.

CUTTING GINGER INTO FINE SLIVERS

Cut a 1-inch knob off a piece of fresh ginger and peel it. Now cut that chunk crossways into the thinnest slices you can manage. Stack 6–7 slices together and cut them crossways into the thinnest slivers possible. Cut all the slices this way. If you need more slivers, start with another knob of ginger.

Potato Chaat

Chaat in India refers to certain kinds of hot-and-sour foods that are generally eaten as snacks but may be served at lunch as well. When I was growing up in Delhi, the servants cooked the main dishes but it was my mother who always made the *chaat,* not in the kitchen but in the pantry where she kept her *chaat* seasonings, the most important of which was roasted and ground cumin seeds. *Chaat* could be made out of many things—various boiled tubers, boiled legumes like chickpeas and mung beans, and even fruit such as bananas, green mangoes, peaches, guavas, and oranges. Chopped cilantro may be sprinkled over the top just before serving.

Serve at room temperature with cold chicken, with kebabs, and, for Indians at least, with tea. Indians love hot tea with spicy snacks.

SERVES 4

1½ pounds waxy boiling potatoes (such as red potatoes), boiled, allowed to cool thoroughly, and peeled (do *not* refrigerate at any point)

1¼ teaspoons salt

¼ teaspoon cayenne pepper, or more, as desired

Freshly ground black pepper, a generous amount

½ teaspoon ground roasted cumin seeds

1½ tablespoons lemon juice

Cut the potatoes into ½-inch dice and put into a glass, ceramic, or stainless-steel bowl. Add all the remaining ingredients and mix well. Taste for balance of spices, adding more of any of the seasonings if you like. Serve at room temperature. (Do not refrigerate. Refrigeration at any stage changes the texture of the potatoes.)

Potato and Pea Chaat

SERVES 4–5

Once the potatoes have been diced into the bowl, add 1 cup boiled and well-drained peas. Add just a little bit more of each of the seasonings, tasting to make sure you have a good balance. Serve at room temperature, with chopped cilantro sprinkled over the top.

Potato Chaat, Stir-Fried

SERVES 4

Make Potato Chaat exactly as the recipe suggests. Then put 3 tablespoons oil in a large well-seasoned or nonstick pan and set on medium-high heat. When hot, put in the potatoes. Stir and fry for 4–5 minutes, until the potatoes are lightly browned. Serve hot, with chopped cilantro sprinkled over the top.

South Indian Potato Curry

A southern potato curry from the Chennai region.

In Chennai, this would be served with rice, and in the north, with a flatbread. *Dal* and vegetables should be added to the meal.

SERVES 4–6

3 tablespoons olive or canola oil

1 teaspoon whole brown mustard seeds

$\frac{1}{2}$ teaspoon *urad dal* or yellow split peas

2 dried hot red chilies

15–20 fresh curry leaves, or 10 fresh basil leaves, torn up

$\frac{1}{2}$ medium onion, chopped

1 medium tomato, chopped

2 teaspoons ground coriander

$\frac{1}{8}$–$\frac{1}{4}$ teaspoon cayenne pepper

1 teaspoon store-bought *garam masala*

1 pound red potatoes, peeled and cut into $\frac{3}{4}$-inch dice

1 teaspoon salt

$\frac{1}{2}$ cup coconut milk from a well-shaken can

4 tablespoons chopped fresh cilantro

Pour the oil into a medium pan and set over medium-high heat. When hot, put in the mustard seeds, *urad dal,* and red chilies. As soon as the mustard seeds begin to pop, a matter of seconds, put in the curry leaves and onions. Turn heat to medium. Stir and fry the onions for about 3 minutes or until they have softened but not browned. Put in the tomatoes, coriander, cayenne, and *garam masala.* Stir for a minute. Add the potatoes and stir a minute. Now pour in 1 cup water and the salt. Bring to a boil. Cover, turn heat to low, and cook 15–20 minutes or until the potatoes are tender. Add the coconut milk and cilantro and stir them in.

Potato and Pea Curry

This is a Delhi/Uttar Pradesh–style dish. I like to use very small, waxy potatoes, each cut in half. If they are larger, you will just have to dice them. The potatoes hold together best if you boil them whole and let them cool at room temperature before you peel and cut them.

We generally serve this curry with Indian flatbreads or with the puffed-up *poori*s. Pickles and chutneys are served alongside. This combination is very popular in North India for breakfast. Sips of hot milky tea ease the spicy potatoes down nicely.

SERVES 4

3 tablespoons olive or canola oil

⅛ teaspoon ground asafetida

¼ teaspoon whole cumin seeds

1 pound small red potatoes, boiled, cooled, peeled, and halved (if potatoes are larger, aim for 1-inch dice)

2 cups peas, fresh or frozen and defrosted

½ cup plain yogurt

1½ teaspoons finely grated peeled fresh ginger

¾ teaspoon salt

¼–½ teaspoon cayenne pepper, or more if you prefer

1 tablespoon ground coriander

Pour the oil into a large, preferably nonstick sauté pan and set over medium-high heat. When hot, put in the asafetida and cumin seeds. Ten seconds later, add the potatoes. Stir and fry until the potatoes have browned lightly. Now put in the peas, 3 tablespoons of the yogurt, the ginger, salt, and cayenne. Stir and cook until the yogurt has been absorbed. Add another 3 tablespoons yogurt and the coriander. Stir and cook until the yogurt is absorbed again. Add the remaining yogurt. Stir and cook for a minute. If you are using frozen peas, the dish is done. If you are using fresh peas, add 3 tablespoons water, cover, turn heat to low, and cook very gently for 6–8 minutes or until the peas are tender.

Spinach with Garlic and Cumin

This is a quick stir-fry, and could be served with most Indian meals.

1½ pounds spinach
3 tablespoons olive or canola oil
1 teaspoon whole cumin seeds

2 cloves garlic, cut into long slivers
½ teaspoon salt
⅛ teaspoon cayenne pepper

Wash the spinach well and chop coarsely. Leave to drain in a colander.

Pour the oil into a wok or a large pan and set over medium-high heat. When hot, put in the cumin. When it sizzles, add the garlic. Stir until the garlic slivers turn golden. Add the spinach, stir, and cover the pan. When the spinach has wilted completely, remove the cover and add the salt and cayenne. Stir and cook on high heat, uncovered, until most of the liquid has boiled away.

Sweet-and-Sour Butternut Squash or Pumpkin

This belongs to a category of Bangladeshi foods known as *bharats.* Part relish and part vegetable dish, they add extra flavor to a meal. We are beginning to find peeled and seeded butternut squash in our supermarkets now, making this dish a snap to make. Those who cannot find it will need to use a peeler to get the skin off. I like to use mustard oil here, as it gives a very Bengali taste to the dish. If you have never used it, this might be a good time to try. Otherwise, use olive oil.

I love this with all pork dishes and at vegetarian meals with other vegetables, *dal,* and *poori*s (a deep-fried flatbread).

SERVES 4–5

3 tablespoons mustard or olive oil

A generous pinch of ground asafetida

$\frac{1}{2}$ teaspoon whole brown or yellow mustard seeds

4 cups ($1\frac{1}{4}$ pounds) peeled and seeded butternut squash or pumpkin, cut into $\frac{3}{4}$–1-inch segments

$\frac{3}{4}$–1 teaspoon salt

$1\frac{1}{2}$ teaspoons sugar

$\frac{1}{8}$–$\frac{1}{4}$ teaspoon cayenne pepper

1 tablespoon plain yogurt

2 tablespoons chopped cilantro

Pour the oil into a frying pan and set over medium heat. When hot, put in the asafetida and mustard seeds. As soon as the mustard seeds start to pop, a matter of seconds, put in the squash. Stir and fry for about 3 minutes or until the pieces just start to brown. Add $\frac{1}{4}$ cup water, cover, turn heat to low, and cook about 10 minutes or until the squash is tender.

Put in the salt, sugar, cayenne, and yogurt. Stir and cook, uncovered, over medium heat, until the yogurt is absorbed and no longer visible. Sprinkle in the cilantro and stir a few times.

Quick Sweet-and-Sour Gujarati Tomato Curry

Here is a dish that takes about 10 minutes to prepare. It is ideally made when tomatoes are in season, but even second-rate, out-of-season tomatoes are given a new life by this very Gujarati mixture of seasonings.

It may be served at a meal with rice, a bean or split-pea dish, vegetables, and relishes. I also love a meal of this curry, Shrimp Biryani, and Spinach with Garlic and Cumin. If you are cooking Western-style grilled pork chops or chicken pieces, just slather this over the top. The combination is marvelous.

SERVES 4–6

3 tablespoons olive or canola oil
$\frac{1}{8}$ teaspoon ground asafetida
1 teaspoon whole black or yellow
    mustard seeds
1 teaspoon whole cumin seeds
2 pounds medium-sized tomatoes,
    quartered

1 teaspoon salt
$\frac{1}{4}$ teaspoon ground turmeric
$\frac{1}{4}$–$\frac{1}{2}$ teaspoon cayenne pepper
2 teaspoons dark brown sugar
1 teaspoon finely grated peeled fresh
    ginger

Pour the oil into a frying pan and set over medium-high heat. When hot, put in the asafetida, mustard seeds, and cumin seeds in the order listed. As soon as the mustard seeds begin to pop, a matter of seconds, put in the tomatoes. Stir once or twice and add the salt, turmeric, and cayenne. Stir and add 3 tablespoons water. Bring to a boil, cover, and cook on medium-high heat for 5 minutes. Stir in the sugar and ginger. Taste, and correct balance of seasonings, if needed. Cover and cook another 2–3 minutes.

Tomato and Onion Curry

I make this curry through the summer, whenever tomatoes over-run the vegetable garden, and then freeze some to last me through the winter.

This may be served as a vegetarian curry at an Indian meal or as a gloppy, spicy sauce to ladle over hamburgers, grilled fish, and baked or boiled potatoes.

SERVES 6 AND MAKES ABOUT 4½ CUPS

3 pounds tomatoes, chopped (about 5 generous cups)
Salt
3 tablespoons olive or canola oil
A generous pinch of ground asafetida
2 teaspoons *urad dal* or yellow split peas
2 teaspoons whole brown or yellow mustard seeds

3 dried hot red chilies
15 fresh curry leaves (use 6 basil leaves, torn up, as a substitute)
1¼ pounds onions, chopped (about 3½ cups)
3 cloves garlic, finely chopped
One 1-inch piece fresh ginger, peeled and finely chopped

Put the tomatoes and 1½ teaspoons salt in a bowl. Mix and set aside until tomatoes give off some liquid.

Pour the oil into a wide, heavy pan and set on medium-high heat. When hot put in the asafetida, *urad dal,* and mustard seeds. As soon as the mustard seeds begin to pop, a matter of seconds, put in the red chilies and, a few seconds later, the curry leaves and onions. Stir and fry the onions for about 10 minutes or until they are translucent, turning the heat down if necessary so they do not brown. Add the garlic and ginger and stir a few times. Add the tomatoes and their liquid and bring to a boil. Turn heat down to medium and simmer vigorously for 35–40 minutes or until the sauce has thickened to a gloppy consistency. Check the salt. You might need to add up to ½ teaspoon more. Remove the whole chilies and serve hot or at room temperature, as preferred.

Pan-Grilled Zucchini

I have not measured out the spices in this recipe, since all you do is sprinkle them over the top. A little more, a little less hardly makes any difference.

Serve this with curries or grilled or baked meats.

SERVES 2–4

4 smallish zucchini, about 1 pound in all

4 tablespoons olive or canola oil

Lemon juice

Salt

Freshly ground black pepper

Ground roasted cumin seeds (page 284)

Cayenne pepper

Cut the zucchini into halves lengthways.

Pour the oil into a large frying pan and set over medium-high heat. When hot, put in the zucchini, skin side down, in a single layer. (Do two batches, if needed.) When the bottom is a reddish brown, turn the pieces over. Brown the second side the same way. Arrange in a single layer in a platter, cut side up. Squeeze some lemon juice over the top. Sprinkle some salt, lots of black pepper, some cumin, and cayenne over the top as well. Serve.

Zucchini and Yellow
Summer Squash with Cumin

Here is how my family in India prepared our everyday summer squash. It was utterly simple and utterly good. The squash itself was different, shaped liked a bowling pin and slightly curled up, but the taste and texture were similar. I like to use yellow squash and zucchini together, but you could use just one or the other.

This dish may be served hot at most Indian meals, and cold as a salad.

SERVES 4–6

$1\frac{1}{2}$ pounds zucchini and yellow squash, combined (2 medium zucchini and 2 medium yellow squash)

4 tablespoons olive or canola oil

A generous pinch of ground asafetida

1 teaspoon whole cumin seeds

1 cup (6 ounces) finely chopped tomatoes

1 teaspoon salt

$\frac{1}{8}$ teaspoon cayenne pepper

Trim the ends of the zucchini and squash and quarter them lengthways. Now cut them crossways into 1-inch segments.

Pour the oil into a frying pan and set on medium heat. When hot, put in the asafetida and cumin seeds. Stir once and then put in the tomatoes. Stir and cook the tomatoes for about 2 minutes or until they have softened and then add all the cut vegetables. Stir and sauté for 2 minutes. Add the salt, cayenne, and $\frac{1}{4}$ cup water. Stir to mix, and bring to a simmer. Cover, turn heat to medium low, and cook, stirring once or twice, for 5–6 minutes or until vegetables are just done.

Sri Lankan White Zucchini Curry

Even though this is called a white curry, it is slightly yellowish in color from the small amount of turmeric in it. In Sri Lanka, it is made with ridge gourd, which looks like a ridged, long, slightly curving cucumber, pointy at the ends. It is sold in Indian, Southeast Asian, and Chinese markets. If you can find it, peel it with a peeler, concentrating mostly on the high ridges, and then cut it crosswise into ¾-inch segments. It cooks in about 3 minutes. I have used zucchini instead because it is just as good and we can all get it easily.

Serve with rice and perhaps Stir-Fried Chettinad Chicken.

SERVES 4–6

4 medium-sized zucchini, about 1½ pounds total, trimmed, cut in half lengthways, and then cut crossways into ¾-inch segments
¼ teaspoon ground turmeric
⅛ teaspoon cayenne pepper
15 fresh curry leaves, lightly crushed in the palm, or 10 fresh basil leaves

½ teaspoon salt
1 medium shallot, peeled and cut into fine slivers
1¼ cups coconut milk from a well-shaken can

Combine all the ingredients in a very large frying pan or sauté pan and set over medium-high heat. Bring to a simmer. Turn heat to medium and cook about 5 minutes, stirring and spooning the sauce over the zucchini.

South Indian Mixed-Vegetable Curry

Known as a vegetable *kurma* in the Tamil Nadu region, there are hundreds of versions of this dish throughout southeastern India. Its basic premise is very simple: you parboil diced vegetables—two vegetables or ten, whatever is in season—drain them, and then dress them with a coconut-yogurt mixture seasoned with spices such as mustard seeds and whole dried chilies. All vegetables are fair game—eggplants, zucchini, squashes, peas, carrots, potatoes, cauliflower, pumpkins.... The motto of this dish seems to be "What have you got? I can use it." It is also quite delicious.

Grated fresh coconut is now sold in a frozen form at most South and Southeast Asian stores. If you wish to use unsweetened, desiccated coconut instead, soak $2\frac{1}{2}$ tablespoons in warm water to barely cover, let that sit for an hour, and then proceed with the recipe.

In the South it is generally eaten at room temperature—balmy—with rice and legumes, but I often serve it in the summer, when my garden is at its most productive, as a salad/vegetable dish that accompanies Indian or Western meats.

SERVES 4

Salt

2 medium carrots (about 6 ounces), peeled and cut into $\frac{1}{2}$-inch dice

1 cup green beans (flat or rounded), cut into $\frac{1}{2}$-inch segments

1 cup peas, fresh or frozen and defrosted

3 tablespoons grated fresh coconut (see note above)

6 tablespoons plain yogurt

$\frac{1}{4}$–$\frac{1}{2}$ teaspoon cayenne pepper

2 tablespoons olive or canola oil

$\frac{1}{2}$ teaspoon whole brown mustard seeds

$\frac{1}{4}$ teaspoon skinned *urad dal* or yellow split peas

1 dried hot red chili

10–15 fresh curry leaves, or 6 basil leaves, torn up

Bring 1 cup water to a boil in a small pan. When boiling, add ½ teaspoon salt and the carrots, beans, and peas. Boil for about 3–4 minutes or until the vegetables are just tender. Drain and put in a bowl.

Combine the coconut, yogurt, cayenne, and ½ teaspoon salt, stirring well to make a sauce. Pour this over the vegetables. Do not mix yet.

Pour the oil into a small frying pan and set over medium-high heat. When hot, put in the mustard seeds, *urad dal,* and red chili. As soon as the mustard seeds begin to pop, a matter of seconds, put in the curry leaves and then pour the oil and spices over the coconut-yogurt dressing. Now mix the vegetables gently with the dressing and spices, and serve warm or at room temperature.

Dal

DRIED BEANS, LEGUMES, SPLIT PEAS

I ndians are hard put to find an all-encompassing English name for what they eat every day in some form—*dal.* Many just call it "lentils" and hope for the best. As a result, you will find *pappadom* labeled "lentil wafers." But for Westerners, lentils conjure up specific images of red, green, brown, and French lentils. Dried beans are never included, nor are chickpeas or split peas.

They are all *dals.*

I have decided to use the word *dal* throughout this book because nothing else will really do. To pronounce the word correctly, just remember that the *a* is a short one, like the one in "calm" and that the *d* is soft, as in "dulce" or "donde" (sorry to resort to other languages). Technically, because the word *dal* comes from *dalna,* or "to split," *dal* really means split peas. But the word has come to stand for the whole family of dried beans and dried peas, both split and whole, skinned and unskinned.

For most Indians, *dal* is a major source of protein, combined as it is often at the table with a grain (usually rice or flatbreads) and either plain yogurt, set at home, or a yogurt relish. The mold of a traditional Indian repast was cast in ancient times and is used to this day. When I was growing up, our family lunch generally contained no meat (unless it was a holiday). What we had was rice or *chapatis,* a *dal,* two vegetables, a salad, and some yogurt. We pretty much ate what all of India was eating. The rice or *chapatis* were the constant. Everything else was varied on a daily basis.

India eats so many *dals* and we cook them in so many different ways: the spicing can be varied; you may cook one *dal* one day and another the next, or *dal*s may be mixed; you could roast split peas before cooking them; you could cook a *dal* with a meat, fish, or vegetable; you could make a dish with a *dal* flour! You can actually go for months and not eat the same *dal* dish twice.

Some of the *dal*s are of Indian origin. *Moong dal* (also called mung beans, and used in East Asia to make sprouts) and the slightly glutinous *urad dal* both have an ancient history in India. Chickpeas and red lentils came via the Middle East but came early. India was growing chickpeas in 2500 BC. *Toor dal* (pigeon peas) may have come from Africa, but could also have developed simultaneously in India.

Many of the whole beans, such as kidney beans in various hues, arrived from the New World with conquering colonialists around the sixteenth century. The colonialists were eventually thrown out, but India kept the beans, just adding them to its already vast collection of *dal*s.

If you were to walk into an Indian *dal* shop, you would find an outstanding variety. First of all, there are the whole beans and peas: whole red kidney beans, large and small, whole black-eyed peas, whole red lentils (*sabut masoor*), whole *urad dal,* whole *moong* beans, whole chickpeas (green, black, beige, large, small), and many more. Then you have most of them in their split forms with skin, as well as their split forms without skin. You also have flours made with nearly all of them, the most popular being the very nutritious chickpea flour.

Almost no South Asian home is without chickpea flour. It is used to make fritters, dumplings, and a whole family of snack foods. It is also used in soupy stews to thicken them, and added to yogurt sauces when they are being heated to prevent curdling. If you want to keep it on hand, store the chickpea flour in the refrigerator.

I remember my mother making fritters on cool monsoon days. She would make a chickpea-flour batter, dip thinly sliced potatoes and cauliflower florets and whole chilies in it, and then deep-fry them all. We would eat these with a green chutney. I try to do the same for my grandchildren. On cold winter days, I make my own thick, droppable batter and dip cut-up shrimp and onions in it. I remove one heaping tea-spoon at a time and drop it into hot oil, frying the fritters until they are a rich, reddish gold! We all sit by the fire and devour them. (See Shrimp and Onion Fritters, page 13 in the appetizer section.)

The normal everyday *dal* is wet and somewhat soupy—its final texture is a personal decision and ranges from the very thin to the very thick. (In India, there is a saying that when guests drop in, you just add more water to the *dal!*) Those eating it with rice take their rice first and then ladle some of the *dal* over it and some to the side, so it can be eaten two ways—mixed with the rice or combined with the vegeta-bles or yogurt or pickles. When eating it with flatbread, it is ladled into small metal bowls known as *katori*s. This way it is easier to scoop it up with the bread. There are exceptions, of course. Black beans (*kali dal*) are generally cooked to be quite thick and are spooned directly onto the plate.

Most *dal*s start out by being washed and then boiled in water until they are tender. They are quite bland at this stage. The transformation comes at the end when oil or *ghee* is heated in a small pan, spices and seasonings are dropped into it until they sizzle, and then all this is poured over the boiled *dal.*

The fresher the *dal,* the faster it cooks. If you have old dried beans that have been sitting around for years, it may be best to throw them away—or be prepared to cook them for hours and hours. *Dal*s are best eaten within a year of being picked and dried. Two-year-old *dal*s are still fine, but they may require longer cooking.

Black Beans

Indian black beans are different from those eaten by much of the Caribbean, Mexico, and Central America. The Indian ones are a very, very dark shade of green but manage to look black. The Central American variety is actually black. However, one may be substituted for the other, even though each has a somewhat different taste and texture.

This is a recipe for dried black beans (Indian or Central American) cooked the way it is done in the villages of the Punjab. Those village homes that have a *tandoor*—a clay oven—leave pots of this *dal* to cook very slowly overnight over the embers.

These beans are usually eaten with whole-wheat flatbreads, vegetables (such as eggplants), and yogurt relishes. They may also be served with rice. Whole-wheat pita bread may be substituted for the Indian flatbreads.

SERVES 6

2 cups Indian or Central American black beans (the Indian ones are sold as whole *urad* with skin or *sabut urad* or *ma ki dal,* and the Central American as *frijoles negros* or just black beans), picked over and washed

2 teaspoons salt, or to taste

2 teaspoons very finely grated peeled fresh ginger

2 cloves garlic, crushed to a pulp

¼ cup chopped fresh cilantro

6 tablespoons tomato paste

¾ cup heavy cream

2 tablespoons unsalted butter

Soak the beans overnight in water that covers them generously. Drain them the next day and put them in a heavy pan along with 6½ cups water. Bring to a boil. Cover partially, lower heat, and simmer very gently for 1½–2 hours or until the beans are tender. (Older beans might take longer to cook.)

Add the salt, ginger, garlic, cilantro, and tomato paste. Stir to mix well and continue to cook on low heat for another 30 minutes. Add the cream and stir in. Just before serving, bring the beans back to a simmer and stir in the butter.

Canned Beans with Indian Spices

Sometimes when I am in a rush and still longing for an Indian *dal,* I take the simple way out and use canned beans—black, great northern, cannellini, or any other beans I like. Today we can get organic canned beans of excellent quality, and it barely takes 15 minutes to cook them. Even the liquid in the can tastes good, so I do not have to throw it away.

Serve these with rice or Indian flatbreads.

SERVES 2–3

2 tablespoons olive or canola oil
A generous pinch of ground asafetida
$\frac{1}{4}$ teaspoon whole cumin seeds
$\frac{1}{2}$ medium onion, cut into fine half
    rings
4 cherry tomatoes, quartered

$\frac{1}{8}$–$\frac{1}{4}$ teaspoon cayenne pepper
$\frac{1}{4}$ teaspoon ground turmeric
One 15-ounce can of black, great
    northern, cannellini, or any other
    beans, preferably organic
About $\frac{1}{2}$ teaspoon salt, as needed

Pour the oil into a small pan and set over medium-high heat. When hot, put in the asafetida and cumin. Let the cumin seeds sizzle for 5 seconds. Add the onions and turn heat to medium. Stir and cook the onions until they have browned a bit. Add the tomatoes and stir a few times. Now add the cayenne and turmeric. Stir once or twice and add the contents of the can (beans and liquid, if organic, otherwise just the beans and the same amount of water as liquid) as well as about 4 tablespoons water. Stir and bring to a simmer. Cover, turn heat to low, and simmer gently for 10 minutes. Add as much salt as needed.

Black-Eyed Peas with Butternut Squash

In India, dried beans and peas may be combined with almost any vegetable. Here, I use either pumpkin or butternut squash. It gives a mellow sweetness to the dish.

In India, this would be eaten with whole-wheat flatbreads, yogurt relishes, salads, and pickles. For a Western meal, the beans may be served with a sliced baguette as a first course or with roast pork or roast lamb.

SERVES 6

2 cups (about 12 ounces) dried black-eyed peas
3 tablespoons olive or canola oil
$\frac{1}{2}$ teaspoon whole cumin seeds
$\frac{1}{2}$ teaspoon whole fennel seeds
1 medium onion, chopped
3 cloves garlic, finely chopped
$\frac{1}{2}$ teaspoon finely chopped peeled fresh ginger
1 fresh hot green chili, chopped

4 tablespoons tomato puree
$1\frac{1}{2}$ teaspoons salt
$\frac{1}{8}$–$\frac{1}{4}$ teaspoon cayenne pepper
$\frac{3}{4}$ pound ($2\frac{1}{2}$ cups) peeled and seeded butternut squash, cut into 1-inch pieces

Soak the black-eyed peas overnight in water that covers them well. Drain.

Pour the oil into a heavy, largish pan and set over medium-high heat. When hot, put in the cumin and fennel seeds. Let them sizzle for 10 seconds and then add the onions. Stir and fry until the onion pieces turn brown at the edges. Add the garlic, ginger, and green chili. Stir for a minute. Add the tomato puree. Stir for a minute. Now put in the peas, salt, cayenne, squash, and $4\frac{1}{2}$ cups water. Bring to a boil. Cover partially, turn heat to low, and cook for about 1 hour or until peas are tender and the water is absorbed.

Chickpeas in a Sauce

There was a time when the easy-to-use canned chickpeas came in such a tin-tasting liquid that they needed not only draining but rinsing as well. The liquid was unusable. Lately, I have found canned organic chickpeas that are in a lovely natural liquid, quite similar to what I get when I boil my own. This is a giant leap, indeed. Look for them.

The chickpeas may be served with Indian flatbreads or rice. Eggplants, greens, and relishes would complete the meal. Meats may always be added.

SERVES 4

3 tablespoons olive or canola oil
¾ teaspoon whole cumin seeds
1 cup (4¼ ounces) finely chopped onions
1 teaspoon finely grated peeled fresh ginger
¾ teaspoon ground coriander
¼–½ teaspoon cayenne pepper
¼ teaspoon ground turmeric

1 cup (4¼ ounces) finely chopped tomatoes
1 teaspoon salt
2½ cups (12½ ounces) cooked, drained chickpeas (save liquid, if from organic can)—a 25-ounce can is about right
½ teaspoon *garam masala*
1 teaspoon lemon juice

Pour the oil into a frying pan and set over medium heat. When hot, put in the cumin seeds. After 10 seconds, put in the onions. Stir and fry until the onions turn brown at the edges. Add the ginger and stir once. Add the coriander, cayenne, and turmeric and stir once. Put in the tomatoes and stir for a minute. Now add 1 cup water and the salt. Bring to a boil. Cover, turn heat to low, and simmer 10 minutes. Add the chickpeas and 1 cup of the chickpea liquid or water. Bring to a boil. Cover, turn heat to low, and cook 15 minutes. Add the *garam masala* and lemon juice. Stir and cook, uncovered, on low heat, another 5 minutes.

Spicy Chickpeas with Potatoes

Here is an everyday dish with a fair number of ingredients. Once you have them all prepared and assembled, the rest is fairly easy. Remember that you can chop the onions in a food processor. I have used two 15-ounce cans of organic chickpeas, draining them to separate the liquid so I can measure it. If you are not using organic canned chickpeas, use water instead of the can liquid. If the can liquid is not enough, add water to get the correct amount.

Serve with Indian or Middle Eastern breads (you can even roll up the chickpeas inside them) with Yogurt Sambol with Tomato and Shallot, page 249, on the side. At a dinner, add meat and a vegetable.

SERVES 6

2 tablespoons ground coriander

2 teaspoons ground cumin

½ teaspoon cayenne pepper

½ teaspoon ground turmeric

4 tablespoons olive or canola oil

½ cup finely chopped red onions or shallots

2 teaspoons finely grated peeled fresh ginger

2 cloves garlic, crushed to a pulp

1 cup finely chopped tomatoes

3¾ cups drained canned chickpeas

1½ cups liquid from can if organic, or water, or mixture of the two

2 medium boiling potatoes (5–6 ounces), peeled and cut into ¾-inch dice

1 teaspoon salt

Mix together the coriander, cumin, cayenne, turmeric, and 3 tablespoons water in a small bowl.

Pour the oil into a medium-sized pan and set over medium heat. When hot, put in the onions. Stir and fry for 3–4 minutes or until lightly browned. Add the ginger and garlic. Stir for a minute. Put in the spice mixture from the bowl. Stir for a few seconds. Add the tomatoes. Stir and cook for about 3 minutes or until the tomato has softened. Add the chickpeas and 1½ cups of the liquid from the can, adding water if needed (see above). Then add the potatoes and the salt. Bring to a boil. Cover, turn heat to low, and simmer gently until the potatoes are tender, about 15–20 minutes.

Chickpeas with Mushrooms

I use cremini mushrooms here since they are very firm, but ordinary white mushrooms will do as well.

You may add finely chopped fresh green chilies (1–2 teaspoons) toward the end of the cooking, as many Indians do, if you want the dish to be hotter.

This may be served at a meal but also makes a wonderful snack as a "wrap" if rolled inside any flatbread. Thinly sliced onions, cilantro, and chopped tomatoes may be rolled inside too. Any chutney from this book or good-quality store-bought salsa could be used instead of the onion-cilantro-tomato mixture.

SERVES 4

¼ cup olive or canola oil
½ teaspoon whole cumin seeds
One 2-inch cinnamon stick
½ medium red onion, finely chopped
2 teaspoons finely grated peeled fresh ginger
1 large clove garlic, crushed to a pulp
10 medium-sized mushrooms (about ½ pound total), cut lengthways into ¼-inch-thick slices

2 teaspoons ground coriander
½ teaspoon ground cumin
¼ teaspoon ground turmeric
½ teaspoon cayenne pepper
½ medium tomato, chopped
2½ cups cooked, drained chickpeas from a can, preferably organic (save liquid)—a 25-ounce can is about right
¾–1 teaspoon salt, or to taste

Pour the oil into a wide pan and set over medium-high heat. When hot, put in the cumin seeds and cinnamon. Let the spices sizzle for a few seconds. Then add the onions. Stir and fry until the edges of the onions brown a bit. Add the ginger and garlic and stir once or twice. Add the mushrooms. Stir until they are wilted. Add the coriander, cumin, turmeric, and cayenne. Stir a few times. Add the tomato and ½ cup of either the chickpea liquid from an organic can or water. Cover, turn heat to low, and cook 10 minutes.

Add the drained chickpeas, salt, and 1 cup of the organic chickpea liquid or water or a mixture of the two. Bring to a simmer. Cover, turn heat to low, and cook gently for 15–20 minutes, stirring now and then.

Karhi, a Yogurt Sauce

Eating a *karhi* is really a way of eating heated yogurt. Because yogurt would curdle into unappetizing blobs if it were to be just heated up, it is stabilized with a flour first. In India, where there are many vegetarians who know that a bean, a grain, and a milk product can make for a balanced meal, it is chickpea flour that is used. Known variously as garbanzo flour, gram flour, chickpea flour, *farine de pois chiches,* and *besan,* it is very nutritious as well as full of a nutty flavor.

Karhis are cooked over much of India with many interesting regional variations.

This yogurt sauce, spicily seasoned and quite scrumptious, is either poured over rice or put into individual bowls and eaten with whole-grain flatbreads. Meats and vegetables are often served on the side.

SERVES 6

¾ cup chickpea flour, sifted

2 cups plain yogurt, preferably the acidophilus yogurt found in health-food stores

3 tablespoons olive or canola oil

1½ teaspoons whole cumin seeds

1½ teaspoons whole brown or yellow mustard seeds

1 teaspoon whole fennel seeds

3 dried hot red chilies

½ teaspoon ground turmeric

About 15 fresh curry leaves or 8 chopped fresh basil leaves

1¾ teaspoons salt

Put the chickpea flour in a large bowl. Very slowly, add 1 cup water, beating with a whisk as you do so. Keep beating until there are no lumps. Add the yogurt and beat it in until the mixture is smooth. Add another 4 cups water gradually, beating as you go.

Pour the oil into a medium pan and set over medium-high heat. When hot, put in the cumin, mustard, and fennel seeds as well as the chilies. As soon as the mustard seeds start to pop, a matter of seconds, put in the turmeric and curry leaves. Stir once and pour in the chickpea-yogurt mixture. Stir with a whisk. Turn heat to medium. Add the salt. Keep stirring with the whisk until the mixture thickens and starts to bubble. Turn heat to low, cover partially, and cook 25 minutes.

Green Lentils with Green Beans and Cilantro

For vegetarians, these refreshing lentils, accompanied perhaps by Yogurt Relish with Okra and a bread, Indian or crusty Western, could make an entire meal. For non-vegetarians, meats or fish curries may be added.

SERVES 4–6

1½ cups green lentils
1 teaspoon salt
¼ teaspoon cayenne pepper
1 cup ¾-inch green bean segments
1 well-packed cup finely chopped
    cilantro

3 tablespoons olive or canola oil
⅛ teaspoon ground asafetida
½ teaspoon whole cumin seeds
1 medium shallot, peeled and cut into
    fine slivers
A few wedges of lemon, if desired

Put the lentils and 4¼ cups water in a medium pan and bring to a boil. Cover partially, turn heat to low, and simmer very gently for 20 minutes. Add the salt, cayenne, green beans, and cilantro. Stir to mix and bring to a boil again. Cover partially and simmer very gently for another 20 minutes. Turn off the heat.

Pour the oil into a small frying pan and set over medium-high heat. When hot, put in the asafetida and cumin seeds. Let the seeds sizzle for 10 seconds. Add the shallots. Stir and fry them on medium heat until they turn reddish. Now pour the entire contents of the frying pan into the pan with the lentils. Stir to mix.

Offer lemon wedges at the table.

OVERLEAF, LEFT: *Green Lentils with Green Beans and Cilantro*
RIGHT: *Bulgar Pilaf with Peas and Tomato*

Red Lentils with Ginger

Red lentils, sold in Indian shops as skinless *masoor dal* and in some places as Egyptian red lentils, usually come in various shades of salmon pink. They originated in the Middle East but came into India quite early and are eaten throughout North India.

This particular dish may be served with most Indian meals. It also happens to be particularly scrumptious over a pasta such as penne or fusilli.

SERVES 4–5

3 cloves garlic, crushed in a garlic press
1 teaspoon finely grated peeled fresh ginger
1 tablespoon ground coriander
1 teaspoon ground cumin
¼ teaspoon cayenne pepper
¼ teaspoon ground turmeric
3 tablespoons olive or canola oil

4 tablespoons chopped onions
1 cup (5 ounces) finely chopped tomatoes
1 cup red lentils (skinless *masoor dal*), washed and drained
¾–1 teaspoon salt
3 tablespoons chopped cilantro
1 tablespoon unsalted butter (optional)

Put the garlic, ginger, coriander, cumin, cayenne, and turmeric into a cup and mix.

Pour the oil into a wide, medium pan and set over medium heat. When hot, put in the onions. Stir and fry until they turn golden at the edges. Add the spice mixture from the cup. Stir for a minute. Add the tomatoes. Stir and cook, scraping the bottom, until the tomatoes have softened. Now put in the red lentils, 3½ cups water, and the salt. Bring to a boil. Cover partially, turn heat to low, and cook 45 minutes. Stir well and cook, uncovered, another 5 minutes. Stir in the cilantro and butter just before serving.

Bangladeshi Red Lentils

An everyday *dal* to be served with rice, vegetables, and curries.
(In Bangladesh, the curry would often be made with fish.)

1 cup red lentils (skinless *masoor dal*), washed and drained

¼ teaspoon ground turmeric

1 medium onion, half finely chopped and half cut into fine half rings

¾–1 teaspoon salt

3 tablespoons olive or canola oil or *ghee*

2 cloves garlic, cut into thin slices

2–3 dried hot red chilies, each broken in half

Put the red lentils, 3½ cups water, turmeric, and the chopped onions into a medium pan. Bring to a boil. Cover partially, turn heat to low, and cook 45 minutes or until the lentils are very tender. Add the salt and mix in.

Pour the oil into a small frying pan set over medium heat. When hot, put in the sliced onions and stir a few times. Add the garlic and chilies. Stir and fry until the onions and garlic have turned a rich golden-red color. Pour the contents of the frying pan into the pot with the *dal.* Stir to mix.

Goan-Style Dal Curry

This delicious *dal* curry may also be made with *moong dal* or an equal mixture of red lentils, *masoor dal,* and *moong dal.* Serve with rice and fish.

SERVES 4–5

1 cup *masoor dal* (red lentils), washed and drained

½ teaspoon ground turmeric

2 medium tomatoes, peeled and chopped

1½ teaspoons salt

1 packed cup (1¾ ounces) chopped cilantro

½–¾ teaspoon cayenne pepper

2 tablespoons olive or canola oil

½ teaspoon whole brown mustard seeds

½ teaspoon whole cumin seeds

½ medium onion, chopped

10–15 fresh curry leaves (if available)

1 teaspoon very finely grated peeled fresh ginger

1 good-sized clove garlic, crushed to a pulp

Put the *dal* and 3 cups water in a medium pan. Bring to a boil but do not let it boil over. Skim off the froth and add the turmeric. Stir, cover partially, turn heat to very low, and simmer gently for 40 minutes. Add the tomatoes, salt, cilantro, and cayenne. Bring to a simmer. Cover, turn heat to low, and simmer 10 minutes. Stir and turn off the heat.

Pour the oil into a small pan or small frying pan and set over medium-high heat. When hot, put in the mustard and cumin seeds. As soon as the mustard seeds begin to pop, a matter of seconds, add the onions and curry leaves. Stir and fry until the onions start to brown. Now put in the ginger and garlic. Stir for a minute and then empty the contents of the small pan into the pan with the *dal.* Stir to mix.

My Everyday Moong Dal

Our family can eat this every single day of the week. It is my soul food.

I love this with Plain Basmati Rice and any vegetable I feel like that day. I also love to add Lemony Ground Lamb with Mint and Cilantro.

SERVES 4–6

1 cup (7 ounces) *moong dal* (hulled and split mung beans), washed and drained
¼ teaspoon ground turmeric
¾ teaspoon salt, or to taste
2 tablespoons olive oil or *ghee*

⅛ teaspoon ground asafetida
½ teaspoon whole cumin seeds
1–2 dried hot red chilies (the short cayenne type)
1 medium shallot, peeled and cut into fine slivers

Put the *dal* in a medium pot and add 3½ cups water. Bring to a boil. Skim off the white froth and add the turmeric. Stir to mix. Cover partially, turn heat to a gentle simmer, and cook 45 minutes. Add the salt and stir to mix. Turn off heat.

Pour the oil into a small frying pan and set over medium-high heat. When hot put in the asafetida, cumin seeds, and chilies, quickly in that order. As soon as the chilies darken, a matter of seconds, add the shallots. Stir and cook until the shallots brown and then quickly pour the contents of the frying pan over the cooked *dal*. Stir to mix.

Roasted Moong Dal with Mustard Greens
(*Bhaja Moong Dal*)

This is a Bengali specialty that requires that the *moong dal* (hulled and split mung beans) be lightly roasted first and then, when the *dal* is almost done, quick-cooking greens such as mustard greens, spinach, or green chard are added to make it more nourishing.

There are several tiny steps required here, but each is simplicity itself. I find that most split peas and beans are so clean these days that they need no picking over. You do need to rinse them off. In the case of this recipe, the rinsing is done after the roasting, for obvious reasons.

Bengalis might use mustard oil for the final seasoning. It complements the mustard greens and adds its own unique flavor. But since it is frowned upon by Western food authorities for the harmful acids it contains, I have started using extra virgin olive oil instead, another strong flavor, though a different one.

For many peasants, such a *dal,* served with rice and perhaps followed by a yogurt dessert, makes for a rich, ample meal. You may add a fish dish.

SERVES 4–6

1 cup (6 ounces) hulled and split
 moong dal
¼ teaspoon ground turmeric
1 tightly packed cup (3 ounces)
 mustard greens, well chopped
 (other tender greens, such as
 spinach or chard, may be
 substituted)

1¼ teaspoons salt
1½ tablespoons extra virgin olive oil
½ teaspoon whole brown or yellow
 mustard seeds
½ teaspoon whole cumin seeds
¼ teaspoon nigella seeds
¼ teaspoon whole fennel seeds
2 dried hot red chilies

Put the unwashed *dal* in a medium pan and set over medium heat. Shake or stir the dal until some of the grains turn a little brown. Now pour cold water into the pan, stir the grains, and pour the water out. Do this one more time. Drain the beans well and add 4 cups fresh water. Add the turmeric and bring to a boil, without letting the *dal* boil over. Cover partially, turn heat to low, and cook 30 minutes. Add the greens and salt. Stir and cook another 20 minutes, with the pan partially covered, stirring now and then.

Heat the oil in a small pan or a small frying pan. When hot, put in the mustard seeds, cumin seeds, nigella seeds, fennel seeds, and chilies, in that order. As soon as the mustard seeds begin to pop, a matter of seconds, pour the oil and seasonings over the cooked *dal,* cover it, and let the flavors blossom for a few minutes before stirring and then serving.

Arhar Dal with Tomato and Onion

The Indian split peas, *arhar dal* and *toovar* (or *toor*) *dal,* are closely related. Both are the hulled and split descendants of the pigeon pea. *Arhar,* the North Indian version, is milder in flavor, whereas *toovar,* used in West and South India, tends to be darker and earthier. Use whichever you can find. If you cannot find either, use yellow split peas.

Serve with rice or Indian flatbreads. Add a vegetable and relishes to complete the meal. Non-vegetarians may add meat or fish, if they like.

SERVES 4–6

1 cup *arhar dal* (or any other split peas), washed and drained
½ teaspoon ground turmeric
1½ teaspoons salt
¼–¾ teaspoon cayenne pepper
3 tablespoons olive or canola oil or *ghee*

½ teaspoon whole cumin seeds
½ teaspoon whole brown mustard seeds
15–20 fresh curry leaves, if available, or 10 fresh basil leaves
1 medium onion, chopped
2 medium tomatoes, chopped

Put the *dal* and 4½ cups water in a medium pan. Bring to a boil and remove the froth that rises to the top. Turn heat to low and add the turmeric. Stir, cover partially, and simmer gently for an hour. Add the salt and cayenne. Stir. Cover partially again and simmer gently for about 10 minutes or until you finish the next step.

Meanwhile, heat the oil in a medium frying pan over medium heat. When it is very hot, put in the cumin and mustard seeds. As soon as the mustard seeds pop, a matter of seconds, add the curry leaves and onions. Stir and fry until the onions have softened a bit and turned brown at the edges. Add the tomatoes and stir on medium-low heat until the tomatoes have softened a bit also, about 2 minutes. Pour the contents of the frying pan into the pan with the *dal* and stir it in.

Toor Dal with Corn

I have only eaten this slightly sweet and slightly sour dish in Gujarat, and how good it was, too. It isn't just corn grains that are cooked in the *dal* but the cob itself, lopped off into reasonably sized rounds. The woody part of the cob flavors the *dal* in mysterious ways. You just cannot pick up these corn pieces with Western cutlery. Hands are required to eat the corn off the *dal*-and-spice-flavored cob sections.

If you cannot find *toor dal* (also labeled *toovar dal* and *arhar dal*), use any other split peas that you can find easily, such as red lentils or yellow split peas. Just remember that red lentils cook faster than *toor dal.*

This *dal* is put into individual serving bowls and served with rice or Indian flatbreads. A selection of other vegetables and relishes are also included in vegetarian meals. Non-vegetarians might add fish or chicken.

SERVES 4–5

1 cup *toor dal* (or any other split peas), washed and drained
¼ teaspoon ground turmeric
1 ear of fresh corn, cut crosswise into 1-inch segments (or as many segments as there are diners)
1¼ teaspoons salt
¼–¾ teaspoon cayenne pepper
1 tablespoon lemon juice

2 teaspoons sugar
2 tablespoons olive or canola oil or *ghee*
⅛ teaspoon ground asafetida
3 whole cloves
½ teaspoon whole cumin seeds
½ teaspoon whole brown mustard seeds
2 whole dried hot red chilies

Put the *dal* and 4 cups water in a medium pan. Bring to a boil and remove the froth that rises to the top. Turn heat to low and add the turmeric. Stir, cover partially, and simmer gently for an hour. Add the corn, salt, cayenne, lemon juice, and sugar. Stir. Cover partially again and simmer gently for 10 minutes.

Heat the oil in a small frying pan. When it is very hot, put in the asafetida, cloves, cumin, mustard seeds, and chilies. As soon as the mustard seeds pop, pour the contents of the frying pan into the pan with the *dal.*

OVERLEAF: *Poori*

Rice and Other Grains

In much of South Asia, grains form the heart of a meal. While Westerners might say, "I feel like roast lamb today, what should I have with it?" most South Asians will just assume that the heart of their meal will be rice, bread, or noodles in some form, depending upon what tradition they were born into. The only question for them would be, "What do I want to complement my grain-based staple with today?"

Let us look at a village in Punjab. This could be Punjab in Pakistan (in its eastern section) or Punjab in India (in its northwestern section). As the Punjabs were once one state in pre-independence India, the food is fairly similar. The staple would be whole-wheat breads made in the *tandoor* or, for breakfast, whole-wheat *paratha*s (griddle breads) made on cast-iron griddles. All families would eat the breads with a *dal,* pickles, perhaps a vegetable, and yogurt. In Pakistan, they might substitute a meat kebab or curry for the vegetable. On special occasions, they would all make a rice pilaf.

Now take a village in South India, Bangladesh, or Sri Lanka where the staple is rice. A mound of rice would be cooked for a family. It would be very plain. It would also be unsalted, ready to absorb flavors from its spicy accompaniments. These might include a fish curry (in Bangladesh, Sri Lanka, and some coastal regions of South India), and certainly a *dal* and yogurt for all the South Indian vegetarians. On special occasions, there would be some flatbreads as well, made out of rice flour or wheat flour. Breakfasts in South India and Sri Lanka might have rice-flour noodles served with fresh cardamom-flavored coconut milk, ground-rice pancakes served with coconut chutney or a *dal,* or other savory, rice-based cakes. Fine rice noodles, freshly made by pushing rice dough through a mold and then steaming the nest that is formed, are very common and eaten at breakfast, lunch, and dinner. At dinner, these might even be served with a fish curry. While it is not easy to make rice noodles at home unless you are well practiced at it, it is very simple to buy dried, East Asian rice sticks and then to just reconstitute them in water. The recipe is on page 224.

Wheat is the basis of more than just flatbreads. A coarse semolina is used throughout South Asia to make sweet halvas and savory pilafs—see page 222 for a Semolina Pilaf with Peas. In the Punjab, I have even had pilafs made out of bulgar wheat, page 221.

In Delhi, my hometown, our main staple was wheat, which we ate in the form of small, delicate *chapatis* (griddle breads) made out of whole-wheat flour. But we also ate rice—basmati rice—at lunchtime. All the meats, vegetables, *dals,* and relishes were first offered with unsalted Plain Basmati Rice, page 207, and then with the *chapatis.* On Sundays we often had a rich meat pilaf for lunch with several vegetables and relishes on the side. Often there were meatballs as well.

Rice can be cooked with almost anything: just some spices and seasonings, or fresh seasonal peas, *dal,* meat, tomato, nuts and dried fruit, shrimp, coconut—whatever you fancy. You will find many such recipes in this chapter.

While South Asians might be addicted to their breads or their rice, all of you cooking from this book can mix and match at will. Do whatever is easy and convenient. If you don't feel up to making flatbreads or rice, eat your curry with a pita bread, a French baguette, a corn tortilla, or a "selice." What is a "selice"? In the inner cities of India and Pakistan, you will find many a citizen, sitting at an outdoor table at a cheap restaurant, scooping up his fiery curry with a "selice" of bread. Yes, that is a slice of loaf bread!

Plain Basmati Rice

Basmati rice is easy to cook if you follow these simple directions: Buy good-quality rice with unbroken grains. The rice should have a pronounced basmati odor. Wash, soak, and drain the rice. Cook it with a light hand without heavy-handed stirring, as the grains can break easily.

This could be an everyday rice when served with a simple *dal,* vegetable, and relish, or a party rice if served with a fish or meat curry.

SERVES 6

2 cups basmati rice

Put the rice in a bowl. Cover with cold water, stirring the rice gently. Pour out the dirty water. Do this 4–5 times. Now cover well with fresh water and leave to soak for 30 minutes (longer will not hurt). Drain and leave in a sieve set over a bowl to drain some more.

Put the drained rice in a heavy pan that has a tight-fitting lid. Add 2⅔ cups water and bring to a boil. Cover tightly, turn heat to very, very low, and simmer gently for 25 minutes.

When ready to serve, remove rice with a slotted spoon, breaking up the lumps gently with the back of the spoon.

Yellow Basmati Rice with Sesame Seeds

Not only does this rice look colorful and taste delicious but the turmeric acts like an antiseptic inside the body and the sesame seeds add a good deal of nutrition.

You can almost eat this by itself. Add a *dal*, perhaps an eggplant dish, and a yogurt relish, and you have a fine vegetarian meal. Or serve with kebabs of any sort and a salad for a light, non-vegetarian meal.

SERVES 4–6

2 cups basmati rice
2 tablespoons olive or canola oil
1 dried hot red chili
1 teaspoon *urad dal* or yellow split peas
1 teaspoon whole brown or yellow
    mustard seeds

1 tablespoon sesame seeds
½ teaspoon ground turmeric
1 teaspoon salt, if desired

Put the rice in a bowl. Wash in several changes of water. Drain. Let the rice soak in water that covers it generously for 30 minutes. Drain through a sieve and leave in the sieve suspended over a bowl to drip.

Pour the oil into a heavy, medium pan (that has a tight-fitting lid) and set over medium-high heat. When hot, put in the red chili, *urad dal,* mustard seeds, and sesame seeds. As soon as the *dal* turns reddish and the mustard seeds begin to pop, add the drained rice, turmeric, and salt. Turn the heat down to medium. Stir very gently and sauté for a minute. Add 2⅔ cups water and bring to a boil. Cover tightly, turn heat to very, very low, and simmer gently for 25 minutes.

Rice Pilaf with Almonds and Raisins

Pilafs may be served at everyday meals but are grand enough for entertaining as well. If you like, you could add a generous pinch of saffron threads to the rice just before you cover it and let it simmer. You could also use chicken stock instead of the 2⅔ cup water.

SERVES 4–6

2 cups basmati rice
3 tablespoons olive or canola oil or
  ghee
One 2-inch cinnamon stick
½ medium onion, sliced into fine half
  rings

2 tablespoons slivered blanched
  almonds
2 tablespoons golden raisins
1 teaspoon salt

Put the rice in a bowl. Wash in several changes of water. Drain. Let the rice soak in water that covers it generously for 30 minutes. Drain through a sieve and leave in the sieve suspended over a bowl to drip.

Pour the oil into a heavy, medium pan (that has a tight-fitting lid) and set over medium-high heat. When hot, put in the cinnamon. Let it sizzle for 10 seconds. Put in the onions. Stir and fry the onions until they start to brown. Add the almonds. Stir until they are golden. Add the raisins. Stir until they are plump, just a few seconds. Add the drained rice and salt. Stir very gently to mix. Add 2⅔ cups water and bring to a boil. Cover tightly, turn heat to very, very low, and simmer gently for 25 minutes.

Sri Lankan Rice with Cilantro and Lemon Grass

Lemon grass is grown on the edges of the more precipitous slopes of Sri Lanka's numerous tea gardens. Some of these plantations are visible from the front patio of Ena's mountain bungalow. Lemon grass keeps insects away, and its long roots hold back the soil.

I had this aromatic and festive dish in the museum-like home of Sri Lankan batik artist Ena de Silva, where it was served with dozens of curries and relishes. You may serve this at banquets and family meals alike. It goes well with coconut-milk-based curries, such as Kerala-Style Chicken Curry.

SERVES 4–6

2 cups basmati rice
3 tablespoons olive or canola oil
3 cardamom pods
3 whole cloves
One 2-inch cinnamon stick
10 fresh curry leaves or 5 fresh basil
    leaves, torn up
2 cloves garlic, crushed to a pulp
2 teaspoons finely grated peeled fresh
    ginger

The bottom 6 inches of a lemon grass
    stalk, cut into 2 pieces
1 packed cup finely chopped cilantro
    (use tender stems and leaves)
2⅔ cups chicken stock
1 teaspoon salt (1½ teaspoons if the
    stock is unsalted)

Wash the rice in several changes of water. Drain. Soak in water to cover generously for 30 minutes. Drain.

Pour the oil into a medium-sized, heavy pan and set on medium-high heat. When hot, put in the cardamom, cloves, and cinnamon. Let them sizzle for 5 seconds. Put in the curry leaves, garlic, ginger, and lemon grass. Stir around for a minute. Add the drained rice and the cilantro. Turn heat to medium and stir for a minute. Add the stock and salt and bring to a boil. Cover tightly, turn heat to very, very low, and cook gently for 25 minutes.

Tomato Pullao

A delicious pilaf that may be served with most Indian meals.

SERVES 6

2 cups basmati rice
1 pound tomatoes, coarsely chopped
About 1 cup chicken stock, if needed
2 tablespoons olive or canola oil
10 whole black peppercorns

5 whole cloves
One 2–3-inch cinnamon stick
2 bay leaves
1 medium onion, cut into fine half rings
1$\frac{1}{2}$ teaspoons salt

Put the rice in a bowl. Cover with cold water, stirring the rice gently. Pour out the dirty water. Do this 4–5 times. Now cover well with fresh water and leave to soak for 30 minutes (longer will not hurt). Drain and leave in a sieve set over a bowl to drain some more.

Put the tomatoes in a blender and liquidize completely. Strain and pour into a measuring jug. Add enough chicken stock or water to make 2$\frac{2}{3}$ cups.

Preheat oven to 325°F.

Pour the oil into a heavy pan and set over medium-high heat. When hot, put in the peppercorns, cloves, cinnamon, and bay leaves. Stir a few times and add the onions. Stir and fry until they turn a reddish color. Add the drained rice. Stir very gently from the bottom for 1 minute. Now add the tomato liquid and salt. Stir and bring to a boil. Cover tightly, first with foil, crimping the edges, and then with the lid. Place in the oven and bake 30 minutes.

Basmati Rice with Lentils

We eat this very nutritious rice dish a lot and frequently serve it to our guests. It is almost a meal in itself, and may be served simply with Karhi, a yogurt sauce, and any vegetable you like.

SERVES 6

$\frac{1}{2}$ cup lentils
2 cups basmati rice
3 tablespoons olive or canola oil
Two 2-inch cinnamon sticks
8 cardamom pods

2 bay leaves
$\frac{1}{2}$ medium onion, cut into fine half
   rings
$1\frac{1}{2}$ teaspoons salt

Soak the lentils in warm water for 3–5 hours. Drain.

Wash the rice in several changes of water. Drain. Soak in fresh water for 30 minutes. Drain.

Pour the oil into a heavy, medium pan (that has a tight-fitting lid) and set over medium-high heat. When hot, put in the cinnamon, cardamom, and bay leaves. Stir for 10 seconds. Put in the onions. Stir and fry until they turn reddish brown. Add the lentils, rice, and salt. Turn heat to medium and sauté rice very gently for a minute. Add 3 cups water and bring to a boil. Cover tightly, turn heat to very, very low, and cook gently for 25 minutes.

Rice with Moong Dal
(Dry Khichri)

One of the oldest Indian dishes and continuously popular these thousands of years is *khichri,* a dish of rice and split peas. (Starting around the Raj period, the British began to serve a version of *khichri* in their country homes for breakast: they removed the *dal,* added fish, and called it kedgeree.) There are two general versions of it: one is dry, like well-cooked rice, where each grain is separate, and the other is wet, like a porridge. Both are delicious. The first is more elegant, the second more soothing. This is the first, the dry version.

Serve it like rice, with all manner of curries.

SERVES 6

1½ cups basmati rice
½ cup hulled and split *moong dal*
3 tablespoons olive or canola oil

½ teaspoon whole cumin seeds
1 small onion, cut into fine half rings
1 teaspoon salt

Combine the rice and *dal.* Wash gently in several changes of water. Drain. Cover generously with fresh water and leave to soak for 2 hours. Drain well.

Pour the oil into a largish, heavy pan and set over medium-high heat. When hot, put in the cumin seeds and, a few seconds later, the onions. Stir and fry until the onions have turned reddish brown. Now add the drained rice and *dal.* Stir very gently for a minute. Add the salt and 2⅔ cups water. Bring to a boil. Cover tightly, turn heat to very, very low, and cook gently for 25 minutes.

Shrimp Biryani

A refreshing rice dish that may be served with vegetables, bean and split-pea dishes, and chutneys. Sometimes, I just eat it all by itself with a large green salad.

SERVES 4–6

2 cups basmati rice

1 pound medium-sized shrimp, peeled and deveined (12 ounces peeled and deveined shrimp)

3 cloves garlic, crushed in a garlic press

1 teaspoon ground cumin

½ teaspoon ground turmeric

¼ teaspoon cayenne pepper, or to taste

Freshly ground black pepper

Salt

3 tablespoons olive or canola oil

4 teaspoons lemon juice

¼ cup chopped fresh cilantro or parsley

4 cardamom pods

2⅔ cups chicken stock

Wash the rice in several changes of water and drain. Cover generously with fresh water and leave to soak for 30 minutes. Drain.

Halve the shrimp crossways. Sprinkle the garlic, cumin, turmeric, cayenne, black pepper, and ⅓ teaspoon salt over the shrimp and rub the seasonings in. Cover and set aside.

Pour the oil into a heavy, medium pan and set over medium-high heat. When hot, put in the shrimp and stir them around for 2–3 minutes or until they are just opaque. Remove with a slotted spoon and put in a bowl. Turn off the heat. Add the lemon juice and cilantro to the bowl of shrimp. Stir to mix and taste for balance of seasonings.

Put the cardamom and chicken stock into the pan used for cooking the shrimp and bring to a boil, scraping the bottom to release the seasonings. Add the drained rice, ½ teaspoon salt if the stock is salted and 1 teaspoon if it is not, and bring to a boil again. Cover tightly, turn heat to very, very low, and cook 25 minutes. Put the shrimp and accumulated juices over the top of the rice, cover quickly, and keep cooking another minute. Turn off the heat. Stir gently to mix and keep covered until needed.

Plain Jasmine Rice

Jasmine rice is very different in texture and taste from basmati rice. It is more clingy, more spongy, and more glutinous and, at its best, has a jasmine-like aroma. On some days it is exactly the soothing rice I yearn for. It is certainly closer to the daily rice eaten in South, East, and West India, where basmati rice is reserved for special occasions only. Look for good-quality jasmine rice, usually sold by Thai and other Oriental grocers. Sadly, price is often a good indication of quality. I usually do not bother to wash it, as I enjoy its slightly sticky quality.

SERVES 4–6

2 cups jasmine rice

Put the rice in a heavy pan along with 3 cups water. Bring to a rolling boil. Cover tightly, turn heat to very, very low, and cook gently for 25 minutes.

Coconut Rice

This is such a soothing rice dish—slightly sweet and salty, with just a hint of black pepper. (Do not eat the peppercorns. Push them to the side of your plate. They are just for flavoring.) As the dish is South Indian, I have made it with jasmine rice, which is closer in texture to the shorter-grained rices commonly found in that region.

I love to serve this with northern lamb and chicken curries, thus breaking tradition and combining north and south in an exciting new way.

SERVES 6

3 tablespoons olive or canola oil
$\frac{1}{2}$ teaspoon whole peppercorns
$\frac{2}{3}$ cup finely sliced shallots
2 cups jasmine rice
$1\frac{1}{2}$ teaspoons salt

$\frac{1}{2}$ teaspoon ground turmeric
$1\frac{1}{2}$ cups coconut milk from a well-shaken can mixed with an equal measure of water

Preheat oven to 325°F.

Pour the oil into a heavy, ovenproof pan and set over medium-high heat. When hot put in the peppercorns. Let them sizzle for a few seconds. Add the shallots and stir-fry until they turn reddish brown. Add the rice, turning heat to low, as well as the salt and turmeric. Stir gently for a minute. Add the coconut milk–water mixture, turn heat to medium high, and bring to a rolling boil. Cover first with foil, crimping the edges, and then with the lid. Place in the oven for 30 minutes. Remove from the oven. Fluff up and mix with a fork and then quickly cover again and leave to rest for 15 minutes.

Yogurt Rice

There are hundreds of versions of this salad-like dish that are eaten throughout South India and parts of western India as well. At its base is rice, the local starch and staple. (Think of the bread soups of Italy and the bread salads of the Middle East.) The rice is cooked so it is quite soft. Then yogurt, and sometimes a little milk as well, is added as well as any fruit (apple, grapes, pomegranate), raw vegetables (diced tomatoes, cucumbers), or lightly blanched vegetables (green beans, zucchini, peas) that one likes. The final step is what makes the salad completely Indian. A tiny amount of oil is heated and spices such as mustard seeds, curry leaves, and red chilies are thrown into it. Then the seasoned oil is poured over the rice salad to give it its pungency and reason for being.

This cooling, soothing dish, somewhat like a risotto, makes a wonderful lunch. It is best served at room temperature, without being refrigerated. Other salads may be added to the meal.

SERVES 4 AS A SALAD AND MANY MORE
AS A TOPPING FOR SOUPS

1 cup jasmine rice

1¼ teaspoons salt

¼ cup cold milk

½ cup plain yogurt (preferably the Greek or acidophilus variety), lightly beaten with a fork or whisk

3–4 cherry tomatoes, quartered and lightly salted

¼ cup finely chopped cilantro

2 teaspoons olive or canola oil

¼ teaspoon *urad dal* (use yellow split peas or lightly crushed raw peanuts as a substitute)

½ teaspoon whole brown mustard seeds

2–3 dried hot red chilies

10 or so fresh curry leaves (optional)

Combine the rice, 3 cups water, and the salt in a medium pan and bring to a boil. Cover tightly, turn heat to very, very low, and cook 25 minutes. Empty rice into a wide bowl and add the milk. Stir to mix and to cool off the rice a bit.

Now add the yogurt and mix again. Add the tomatoes and cilantro and mix them together.

Put the oil in a small pan or frying pan and set over medium-high heat. When hot, put in the *urad dal.* Let it turn reddish. Put in the mustard seeds and chilies. As soon as the mustard seeds pop and the chilies darken, add the curry leaves. A second later, pour the oil and spices over the yogurt-rice mixture. Stir to mix.

Plain Brown Rice

South Asians do not really eat brown rice, but many people in South India, western coastal India, and Sri Lanka enjoy a very nutritious red rice. The grains have a red hull that is only partially milled. This is eaten plain and also ground into flour to make pancakes and noodles.

This recipe works for all the brown rices available in the West, and may be served with all South Asian meals.

SERVES 3–4

1 cup brown rice
$\frac{1}{2}$ teaspoon salt, if wanted

Put the rice, 2 cups water, and salt in a small, heavy pan with a tight-fitting lid. Bring to a boil uncovered. Cover tightly, turn heat to very, very low, and cook for 45 minutes. Take covered pan off the heat and leave for 10 minutes.

Curried Brown Rice

Here is a recipe I have devised for the brown rices (and mixtures that combine brown rice with wild rice) usually found in Western markets.

Served with vegetables and a yogurt relish, it makes a fine vegetarian meal. You may also serve this with meat and fish curries.

SERVES 3–4

2 tablespoons olive or canola oil
4 cardamom pods
One 2-inch cinnamon stick
5 tablespoons chopped onions
$\frac{1}{8}$ teaspoon ground turmeric

$\frac{1}{2}$ teaspoon ground cumin
$\frac{1}{8}$ teaspoon cayenne pepper
1 cup brown rice
2 cups chicken stock or vegetable stock
Salt

Pour the oil into a small, heavy pan and set over medium-high heat. When hot, put in the cardamom and cinnamon. Stir once or twice and add the onions. Stir and fry until the onions turn brown at the edges. Lower heat to medium and put in the turmeric, cumin, and cayenne. Stir once and add the rice, stock, and $\frac{1}{4}$ teaspoon salt if the stock is salted, $\frac{1}{2}$ teaspoon if it is not. Stir and bring to a boil. Cover tightly, turn heat to very, very low, and cook for 45 minutes. Take covered pan off the heat and leave for 10 minutes.

Bulgar Pilaf with Peas and Tomato

Bulgar, a wheat that has been cooked, cracked, and dried, is used in parts of the Punjab (northwestern India) to make a variety of nutritious pilafs. The coarser-grained bulgar is ideal here.
Serve as you would a rice pilaf.

SERVES 4

3 tablespoons olive or canola oil
½ teaspoon whole cumin seeds
1 teaspoon very finely grated peeled
    fresh ginger
1 medium tomato, very finely chopped

1 cup peas, fresh or frozen and
    defrosted
1 cup coarse bulgar wheat
¼ teaspoon cayenne pepper
¾ teaspoon salt

Pour the oil into a smallish but heavy pan with a tight-fitting lid and set on medium-high heat. When hot, put in the cumin seeds. Ten seconds later, put in the ginger. Stir once and add the tomatoes. Stir for a minute and add the peas, bulgar, cayenne, and salt. Turn heat to medium and stir gently for a minute. Add 1½ cups water and bring to a simmer. Cover tightly, turn heat to very, very low, and cook gently for 35 minutes. Turn off the heat. Lift the lid and quickly put a dish towel over the pilaf. Cover again with the lid and leave in a warm place for 20 minutes, allowing the towel to absorb some of the moisture. Fluff up and serve.

Semolina Pilaf with Peas

Here is one of the great offerings from Kerala, a state on the southwest coast of India, where it is known as *uppama.* The semolina that is required here is a coarse-grained variety that is sold as *sooji* or *rava* in the Indian stores or as 10-minute Cream of Wheat in the supermarkets. (It is not the very fine version used to make pasta.)

This pilaf-like dish may be eaten as a snack with tea, for breakfast with milky coffee and an accompanying coconut chutney (see Sri Lankan Cooked Coconut Chutney), or as part of a meal as the exquisite starch.

SERVES 3–4

1 cup peas, fresh or frozen and defrosted
Salt
2 tablespoons olive or canola oil
⅛ teaspoon ground asafetida
½ teaspoon *urad dal* or yellow split peas
½ teaspoon whole brown mustard seeds
10 fresh curry leaves, or use 5 basil leaves

½ teaspoon very finely grated peeled fresh ginger
2–4 fresh hot green chilies (such as bird's-eye), finely chopped
1 cup (6 ounces) semolina (see above)
2 tablespoons finely chopped cilantro
2 teaspoons lemon juice
1 teaspoon sugar

Boil the peas with a little salt long enough to just cook them and then drain.

Put 2 cups water in a small pot and bring to a boil. Turn heat to very low and leave.

Pour the oil into a nonstick frying pan and set over medium-high heat. When hot, put in the asafetida and *urad dal.* Wait 2 seconds and put in the mustard seeds. As soon as the *dal* turns red and the mustard seeds pop, a matter of seconds, put in the curry leaves, ginger, and chilies. Stir for a few seconds and add the semolina and 1 teaspoon salt. Stir and cook for 3–4 minutes or until the semolina is very lightly browned. Turn heat to low. Now begin to add the boiling water a few tablespoons at a time over the next 7 minutes (just pour it from the pan), stirring and breaking up the lumps as you do so. Add the peas and cilantro. Keep cooking and stirring on very low heat another 3–4 minutes or until all the grains puff up. Add the lemon juice and sugar and stir to mix.

Thin Rice Noodles/Idiappam/ Rice Sticks

Throughout southern India and Sri Lanka fine, homemade, steamed rice noodles are often served at mealtimes instead of rice and are known as *idiappam* (or string hoppers) in India and *idiappa* in Sri Lanka. Since making them is somewhat cumbersome, requiring a special mold and steaming equipment, I do the next best thing: I buy dried rice sticks from East Asian grocers and reconstitute them.

These noodles could be served at breakfast with a little sugar and cardamom-flavored coconut milk and at major meals with curries—though in Sri Lanka I have had them with fish curries for breakfast to my great delight, and with fiery fish curries in Kerala for dinner.

SERVES 4

6 ounces dried rice sticks

Soak the rice sticks in a large bowl of water that covers them completely for 2–3 hours. Shortly before eating, drain them and put them back in the bowl. With a pair of kitchen scissors, snip the noodles into manageable lengths. Pour boiling water over them. Leave for a minute and drain.

Thin Rice Noodles with Brussels Sprouts

This South Indian–style dish may also be made with shredded cabbage. Dried rice sticks are sold by East Asian grocers. You will notice that a little raw rice is used here as a seasoning. It provides a nutty texture.

Serve with a lamb or beef curry or grilled meats.

SERVES 4

6 ounces dried rice sticks

8 ounces Brussels sprouts

2 tablespoons olive or canola oil

$\frac{1}{2}$ teaspoon any raw white rice

$\frac{1}{2}$ teaspoon whole brown mustard
  seeds

4 dried hot red chilies

10–15 fresh curry leaves or 5 fresh
  basil leaves

1 teaspoon salt

Soak the rice sticks in a bowl of cold water for 2–3 hours. Take a pair of kitchen scissors and snip the noodles, shortening them so they can be lifted up easily. Drain and leave in the strainer.

Trim the sprouts. Cut each in half lengthways and then crossways into $\frac{1}{4}$-inch-thick shreds.

Pour the oil into a nonstick frying pan and set on medium-high heat. When hot, put in the rice. Five seconds later, add the mustard seeds and chilies. As soon as the mustard seeds start to pop, add the curry leaves and the sprouts. Stir and fry the sprouts for 5 minutes or until they are lightly browned. Add $\frac{1}{2}$ cup water and cover. Turn heat to low and cook 1 minute. Add the rice noodles and salt. Stir for 3–4 minutes. Add 1 cup water and bring to a simmer. Cover and cook on very low heat for 5 minutes, stirring frequently.

Chapati (Whole-Wheat Flatbread)

A *chapati* is like a tortilla. Unlike a corn tortilla, it is made out of wheat flour. Unlike a wheat tortilla, it is made out of whole-wheat flour known as *ata* or *chapati* flour. You may use a tortilla press or a *chapati* press (they are almost the same) instead of rolling each one out with a rolling pin. Small thin *chapati*s (about 5 inches in diameter) are considered much more elegant than large thick ones, though you will find all sizes in the cities and villages of India.

Those who eat *chapati*s daily eat them with everything at lunch and dinner. You break off a piece and enfold a piece of meat or vegetable in it. If you want to spice up the morsel a bit more, you brush it against a chutney or pickle. You could also roll up some food inside a whole *chapati*, to make a kind of "wrap," though you would not do this at the table, only with leftovers to make a snack.

MAKES 6

1 cup *chapati* flour or whole-wheat pastry flour, plus extra for dusting

Butter or *ghee* to put on top of *chapati*s, if desired

Make a soft dough using all the flour and about ½ cup water. Knead well for 10 minutes. Make a ball and put it in a plastic bag or in a bowl covered with a damp cloth. Leave for at least 15–30 minutes or refrigerate it for future use.

Set a cast-iron frying pan (an iron crepe pan is also good) over medium-high heat and allow to heat up.

Knead the dough again and then divide it into 6 balls. Keep 5 covered. Dust your work surface with the extra flour when needed and roll the sixth ball out evenly into a 5¼-inch round. Pick the *chapati* up and slap it around between your two palms to dust off some of the extra flour. Now slap it onto the hot pan. Cook for 10 seconds. Flip it over. Cook the second side for 10 seconds. Flip it over a second time and cook for 10 seconds. Flip it a third time and cook 10 seconds. Now pick up the *chapati* and put it in your microwave oven. Blast it for about 30 seconds or until puffed. (If you have no microwave, press down on different parts of the *chapati* with a small wad of cloth as you give it a slight turn in the pan.) Remove, brush with butter or *ghee,* if desired, and keep covered while you make the rest.

Using a slightly damp paper towel, wipe off the frying pan. Turn the heat down to medium low while you roll out your second *chapati* and proceed as before, turning the heat up again before you slap the next *chapati* onto the hot surface.

Poori (Deep-Fried Puffed Bread)

A *poori* requires almost the same dough as the *chapati*, except there is a little oil in it. It is rolled out almost the same way too, but then, instead of being cooked on a hot, griddle-like surface, it is deep-fried quickly in hot oil, making it puff up like a balloon. (When the same bread is made with white flour, as it is in Bengal, it is called a *loochi*.)

*Poori*s may be eaten with all curries and vegetables. At breakfast, *pooris* are often served with potato dishes—such as Potato and Pea Curry or Potatoes with Cumin and Mustard Seeds—and hot pickles and chutneys. They are eaten very much like *chapatis*—you break off a piece and roll some vegetable in it, then brush it against a pickle or chutney. We always took them on picnics with us, all stacked up inside a tin. On picnics and train journeys, they were eaten with ground-meat dishes and pickles, all at room temperature.

MAKES 12

2 cups *chapati* flour or whole-wheat pastry flour
½ teaspoon salt

1 tablespoon olive or canola oil for the dough plus more for deep-frying and rubbing on dough
About 1 cup milk or water

Put the flour and salt into a bowl. Dribble in the 1 tablespoon oil and rub it into the flour. Slowly add enough milk or water so you can gather all the dough together into a ball. Knead the dough for 10 minutes until smooth. Make a ball. Rub the ball with a little oil and slip it into a Ziploc or other plastic bag and leave for 30 minutes.

Pour oil for deep-frying into a wok, *karhai,* or frying pan and set on medium heat. In a wok or *karhai,* the oil should extend over a diameter of at least 6 inches. In a frying pan, you will need at least 1 inch of oil. Allow it time to heat up. Keep a large baking tray lined with paper towels next to you.

Meanwhile knead the dough again and divide it into 12 balls. Keep 11 covered. Take the twelfth ball and rub it lightly with oil. Now flatten it into a patty and roll it out into a 5–5½-inch round. Lift the round and fearlessly lay it on top of the hot oil without allowing it to fold up. It may sink, but should rise to the surface almost immediately. Now, using the back of a slotted spoon, keep pushing the *poori* under the surface of the oil with rapid, light strokes. It will resist and puff up in seconds. Turn it over and count to 2. Now lift the *poori* out of the oil and deposit it on top of the paper towels. Make all the *poori*s this way. Stack and cover tightly in foil if not eating right away.

Paratha (Griddle Bread)

The dough for the *paratha* is similar to that of a *poori* but is rolled out very differently to give it multiple layers. It is cooked on a cast-iron griddle rather like a pancake, with butter, *ghee,* or oil to keep it lubricated. This particular *paratha,* among the simplest to make, is triangular in shape.

*Paratha*s are a very popular breakfast food when they are eaten with yogurt and pickles. They may also be served at mealtimes with meats and vegetables.

MAKES 8

1½ cups *chapati* flour or whole-wheat pastry flour
½ teaspoon salt
1 tablespoon olive or canola oil plus a little more

About ¼ cup melted butter or melted *ghee*

Put the flour and salt into a bowl. Dribble in the oil and rub it in with your fingertips. Slowly add about ½ cup or more water and gather all the flour together. You are aiming for a soft dough. Knead for 8–10 minutes. Form into a ball. Rub it with oil and slip it into a plastic bag for 30 minutes.

Set a cast-iron griddle or cast-iron frying pan over medium heat. While it heats, knead the dough again and divide it into 8 even balls. Keep 7 covered as you work with the eighth. Flatten it a bit and, on a floured surface, roll it out into a 5-inch round. Brush the surface with butter/*ghee* and fold in half. Brush the top with the butter/*ghee* again and fold in half again, forming a triangle. Roll out the triangle on a floured surface, keeping its basic shape, until the three sides are about 5 inches long. Brush the griddle with butter/*ghee* and slap the *paratha* onto it. As soon as one side is golden, turn it over and add a little more butter/ghee. A few dark spots are fine. Adjust the heat, if needed. Do not let the *paratha* turn brittle. Remove and wrap in foil. Make all the *paratha*s this way. The foil bundle may be reheated in a medium oven, or individual *paratha*s may be heated for about 30 seconds each in a microwave oven.

Relishes

LITTLE SALADS, CHUTNEYS,
AND PICKLES

and Some Drinks

South Asians demand a lot of their meals: they want them to be soothing, comforting, and nourishing; they insist upon contrasting flavors and textures; they also expect that every mouthful will be full of titillating, varying possibilities.

The last is achieved with the relishes that are served with every single meal. "Relish" is a wide, loose term. Think of the pickles served at a Jewish New York delicatessen or the mustard and horseradish served with English roast beef or the rouille served with a French fish soup. They all add "a little something," a little pep. South Asians often have more than one such item at the table. The reasons are partly nutritional—yogurt relishes supply protein, fresh chutneys made from herbs or tamarind add vitamins and iron, and fresh salads provide roughage.

But there is more to it than that. This part of the world likes each mouthful to have the possibilities of variation. Individuals might decide not to exercise that option. But they want it available to them.

Hence all the relishes at the table. Not all are made that day. The pickles might have been put up months earlier or just bought; the sweet, preserve-type chutneys might be sitting in the storeroom or may also have been bought; all that needs to be prepared on the same day is the yogurt relish and the fresh green or red chutney and the salad, which could be as basic as sliced raw onions with tomatoes and cucumbers.

Even if you are poor and eating a very simple meal of rice/bread and beans, you can add a little yogurt to one mouthful, a little pickle to the next, a bit of salad—which could be just sliced onions—to the third, and some fresh chutney to the fourth. The world is your oyster. You are now a king, or queen, in your own home!

LEFT: *Bengali-Style Tomato Chutney* TOP RIGHT: *Peshawari Red Pepper Chutney* LOWER RIGHT: *Green Chutney*

Salaad

My North Indian family called this *salaad,* or salad, but similar salads with varying seasonings are known in some parts of India as *cachumbar.* These salads generally contain onions (our Indian red onions), cucumbers, and tomatoes but, according to the seasons, we in Delhi could find radishes or kohlrabi in them as well. In some parts of India, barely sprouted mung beans and peanuts could be added. This fresh salad was always at our table at every meal in some form, with the simplest of dressings added at the last minute. There was never any oil in this dressing. Instead, there was fresh lime juice, salt, pepper, chili powder, and ground roasted cumin seeds. We just put a generous dollop on our plates (or side plates) and ate it with everything.

SERVES 4

1 cup (5 ounces) peeled cucumbers cut into $\frac{1}{3}$-inch dice

7 large cherry tomatoes, quartered (or use 12 smaller tomatoes and just halve them)

1 good-sized shallot, peeled and cut into fine slivers

$\frac{1}{2}$ teaspoon salt

Freshly ground black pepper

$\frac{1}{2}$ teaspoon ground roasted cumin seeds (see page 284)

$\frac{1}{8}$ teaspoon cayenne pepper

1 tablespoon lime or lemon juice

Mix the cucumbers, tomatoes, and shallots together in a bowl. Just before serving add the salt, pepper, cumin, cayenne, and lemon juice. Toss to mix.

Cucumber Salad, North Indian Style

In much of India, a fresh salad is present at every single meal. This kind of cucumber salad was something that my mother threw together moments before we sat down to eat. Cucumbers with tiny undeveloped seeds have the best texture, but when cucumbers are growing wildly in my garden and some that hid themselves too successfully among the leaves have grown beyond the best picking size, I pick them anyway, peel them, and scoop out their seeds. They still make good eating.

(Whenever I pick a particularly large, overgrown cucumber, I can never throw it in the compost heap because I think of Inder Dutt. At the age of thirteen, he came down from a poor village in the Himalayan mountains to try to eke out a living in the plains. In Delhi, he somehow managed to get into a cousin's household where they taught him how to do odd jobs and eventually even how to cook. He became so adept that my cousin brought him to New York as her cook. Every now and then he would come over to our apartment to help out. I could never get enough of the stories about his childhood. He had spent the snowy mountain winters without shoes, huddling in the floor above the animals to stay warm at night. In the summers, he had to go work in the fields. When he got very thirsty, he would just pick the largest cucumber he could find, snap it in two, and quench his thirst with its juicy flesh.)

SERVES 4–6

3 cups cucumbers (after slicing)
¾ teaspoon salt
Freshly ground black pepper

¼ teaspoon ground cayenne pepper or finely crushed red pepper
1–2 teaspoons lemon juice
8–10 fresh mint leaves, chopped

If you have large, waxed cucumbers, peel them. Otherwise, leave them unpeeled. Cut cucumbers in half lengthways (not necessary if the cucumbers are very slim). Then cut crossways into thin slices or chunks, as desired. Add remaining ingredients. Toss to mix and taste. Adjust seasonings as needed.

TOP: *Peach Salad*
MIDDLE: *Yogurt Relish with Spinach*
BOTTOM: *Cucumber Salad*

Peach Salad

There were many salad-like dishes made with seasonal fruit that my mother served with our lunches. If guavas were in season, they were pressed into service; it could also be star fruit, bananas, peaches, green mangoes, whatever was available in abundance. The seasonings in these salads did not vary much— salt, pepper, ground roasted cumin, Indian chili powders, made from red chilies and sometimes yellow chilies as well, sugar as needed, and lime juice. My mother made the salads herself, not in the kitchen but in the pantry and at the very last minute, just as we sat down to eat, so the fruit would not start "weeping" and get all watery.

The seasoning amounts given in this recipe are approximate, since the taste of fruit can vary so much. Keep tasting as you go, adding more or less of the seasonings, as desired.

SERVES 2–3

2 ripe peaches, peeled, pitted, and cut into about 10 slices each
$\frac{1}{4}$ teaspoon salt (you will need a bit more, but start with that)
Freshly ground black pepper
$\frac{1}{2}$ teaspoon ground roasted cumin seeds

$\frac{1}{8}$ teaspoon cayenne pepper
2 teaspoons sugar
2 teaspoons lemon juice
2 teaspoons finely chopped cilantro or fresh mint

Just before eating, put all ingredients into a bowl and toss.

Thin Raw Onion Rings

Indians love raw onion rings with their kebabs, just as Americans like a slice of onion with their hamburgers. Browned meat and raw onions—it is a marriage made in heaven. The Indian rings are different, though. They are made from smaller onions and are cut paper thin. To temper the sharpness, they are soaked in cold water and dried off thoroughly in a towel. The rings separate, leaving a mound of tangled rings.

SERVES 4–6

2 medium onions

Peel the onions and cut them crosswise into the finest rings possible. Soak them in a bowl of icy water for 30 minutes. Drain well and dry thoroughly in a tea towel, twisting the towel if needed.

Cauliflower Cachumbar

This is a salad from India's western state of Gujarat. Two table-spoons of crushed roasted peanuts could be added to it just before serving and stirred in. It may be served with most Indian meals and lasts several days in the refrigerator if kept covered.

SERVES 4

3 cups (9 ounces) chopped cauliflower (chop it so no piece is larger than $\frac{1}{3}$" × $\frac{1}{4}$")
1 teaspoon salt
$\frac{1}{2}$ teaspoon cayenne pepper
1 teaspoon finely chopped hot green chili, such as bird's-eye, green cayenne, or jalapeño

3–4 tablespoons chopped cilantro
$\frac{1}{2}$ teaspoon sugar
2 tablespoons lemon juice
2 teaspoons wine vinegar (red or white)
1 tablespoon olive or canola oil
$\frac{1}{2}$ teaspoon whole brown or yellow mustard seeds

Put the cauliflower in a bowl. Add the salt and rub it in, mixing well. Let macerate for 1–3 hours.

If any liquid has accumulated, drain it. Add the cayenne, chilies, cilantro, sugar, lemon juice, and vinegar. Mix.

Put the oil in a small pan and set over medium-high heat. When hot, put in the mustard seeds. As soon as the seeds begin to pop, a matter of seconds, pour the contents of the pan over the cauliflower. Stir to mix.

Okra Sambol

This Sri Lankan *sambol* may best be described as an accompanying salad or relish to be served at curry meals. You can make it as hot as you like.

SERVES 3

3 tablespoons olive or canola oil

½ pound okra, top and tail removed and cut crossways into ½-inch pieces

⅓ cup (1½ ounces) red onion, cut into very fine half rings (if the onion is large, cut into quarter rings)

½–¾ teaspoon salt

⅛–¼ teaspoon cayenne pepper

Freshly ground black pepper

2–3 teaspoons lemon juice

Pour the oil into a frying pan and set over medium-high heat. When hot, put in the cut okra. Stir and fry for 6–7 minutes or until okra is lightly browned. Remove with a slotted spoon and put in a bowl. Add all the remaining ingredients to the bowl. Mix well and taste, adjusting to get the perfect balance.

Vinegar-Chili-Onion Dipping Sauce

This simple sauce is perfect for spooning over fried fish, fried chicken, grilled meats, and any kind of kebab.

SERVES 2–3

2 tablespoons red wine vinegar (or any vinegar you like)
1 tablespoon very finely slivered shallots or a couple of very thin onion slices, quartered

$\frac{1}{8}$ teaspoon cayenne pepper
$\frac{1}{8}$–$\frac{1}{4}$ teaspoon salt
6–8 mint leaves, finely chopped (optional)

Mix all the ingredients together in a small bowl and leave for 30 minutes to steep.

Peshawari Red Pepper Chutney

This hot, savory chutney is from what used to be India's north-west frontier but now is on Pakistan's border with Afghanistan. There it is made with fresh red chilies, which have beautiful color and medium heat. They are not always easy to find, so I use a mixture of red bell peppers and cayenne pepper. They are always combined with nuts, generally almonds but sometimes walnuts. This chutney may be frozen. It is like gold in the bank. Serve it with kebabs, fritters, and with a general meal.

SERVES 8

$\frac{1}{2}$ large red bell pepper, seeded and
   coarsely chopped
20 large fresh mint leaves or 30 smaller
   ones, coarsely chopped
2 tablespoons lemon juice
1 clove garlic, coarsely chopped

$\frac{1}{2}$ teaspoon cayenne pepper
$\frac{1}{2}$ teaspoon salt
Freshly ground black pepper
1 tablespoon slivered blanched
    almonds or chopped walnuts
1 teaspoon chopped fresh dill

Put the red bell pepper, mint, lemon juice, garlic, cayenne, salt, and black pepper into a blender in the order listed and blend until smooth. Add the almonds and blend again. Pour into a bowl and check for seasonings. Mix in the dill.

Bengali-Style Tomato Chutney

At Bengali banquets, this chutney, along with deep-fried, puffed white-flour breads (*loochi*s) and *pappadoms*, is served as the penultimate course, just before the dessert. Here in the Western world, I tend to serve it with the main meal: I layer it thickly on hamburgers, serve dollops with fried chicken and roast lamb, use it as a spread for cheese sandwiches, and, at Indian meals, offer it as a relish with my kebabs and curries.

MAKES A GENEROUS $1\frac{1}{2}$ CUPS

2 tablespoons olive, canola, or peanut oil
$\frac{1}{2}$ teaspoon whole cumin seeds
$\frac{1}{2}$ teaspoon whole brown or yellow mustard seeds
$\frac{1}{4}$ teaspoon whole fennel seeds
2 cups tomato puree, canned or homemade

$1\frac{1}{2}$ teaspoons very finely grated peeled fresh ginger
$\frac{3}{4}$ cup apple cider vinegar
1 cup sugar
$\frac{3}{4}$ teaspoon red pepper flakes
$1\frac{1}{4}$ teaspoons salt
2 tablespoons golden raisins (optional)

Pour the oil into a heavy, medium, stainless steel pan and set over medium-high heat. When hot, put in the cumin and mustard seeds. As soon as the mustard seeds begin to pop, a matter of seconds, add the fennel seeds. A few seconds later, put in the tomato puree, ginger, vinegar, sugar, pepper flakes, and salt. Stir and bring to a simmer. Once bubbling, turn heat down to low and cook, uncovered, stirring now and then, for about 50 minutes. Add the raisins and cook another 10 minutes. The chutney should be thick and have a glazed appearance. Put the chutney into a jar, allow to cool, and then screw the lid on and refrigerate.

Fresh Green Chutney

A fresh chutney to serve with all Indian meals, it has a shelf life
of 2–3 days if stored in the refrigerator. What is not used up
may be easily frozen for another day.

SERVES 8

4 teaspoons lime or lemon juice
1 smallish (3-ounce) tomato, chopped
$\frac{3}{4}$ teaspoon salt
3 fresh hot green chilies (such as bird's-
   eye), chopped

$\frac{1}{2}$ cup chopped cilantro
20 fresh mint leaves
$\frac{1}{2}$ cup grated coconut, fresh or frozen
   and defrosted

Put 3 tablespoons water, the lime juice, tomatoes, salt, and chilies into a
blender. Blend thoroughly. Add the cilantro and mint. Blend again until
smooth. Finally, add the coconut and blend some more, pushing down with a
rubber spatula if necessary, until the chutney is smooth.

Sri Lankan Coconut Sambol

This is Sri Lanka's everyday coconut *sambol.* Known as *pol sambol,* it would be called a chutney in India. It may be served with any meal.

SERVES 6

1 tablespoon lime or lemon juice
$\frac{1}{2}$ teaspoon salt
$1\frac{1}{2}$ teaspoons cayenne pepper

1 teaspoon paprika
$\frac{1}{2}$ cup grated coconut, fresh or frozen
  and defrosted

Put $\frac{1}{2}$ cup plus 2 tablespoons water into a blender. Add all the ingredients in the order listed and blend until you have a smooth paste.

Sri Lankan Cooked Coconut Chutney

This delightful chutney is served with all manner of savory steamed rice cakes and pancakes. I love it with the Semolina Pilaf on page 222, but it may be served with most Indian meals. Store in the refrigerator 2–3 days or freeze leftovers.

SERVES 6–8

1 tablespoon lime or lemon juice

2 cloves garlic, chopped

$\frac{1}{2}$ teaspoon salt

3 fresh hot green chilies (such as bird's-eye), chopped

$\frac{1}{4}$ teaspoon whole cumin seeds

1 medium shallot, one half chopped, the other half cut into fine slivers

10–15 fresh curry leaves plus another 10 later (omit if unavailable)

$\frac{1}{2}$ cup grated coconut, fresh or frozen and defrosted

1 tablespoon olive or canola oil

$\frac{1}{4}$ teaspoon whole brown mustard seeds

Put $\frac{1}{2}$ cup water, the lime juice, garlic, salt, chilies, cumin, chopped shallots, and the 10–15 curry leaves into a blender in the order listed and blend thoroughly. Add the coconut and blend thoroughly again.

Put the oil in a small pan and set over medium heat. When hot, scatter in the mustard seeds. As soon as the mustard seeds pop, a matter of seconds, add the 10 curry leaves and the sliced shallots. Stir and cook until the shallots soften slightly and then add the contents of the blender into the pan. Stir and bring to a simmer. Simmer very gently for a minute and turn off the heat. Serve warm or at room temperature.

Peanut Chutney with Sesame Seeds

This may be served with all Indian meals. It is particularly good with grilled meats and kebabs and makes an exciting dip for vegetables and all manner of crisps and fritters. Also, try a layer of it in a sandwich (cheese, turkey, or tomato-and-lettuce) instead of butter.

MAKES ABOUT 7–8 TABLESPOONS

2 tablespoons unsalted peanut butter (if salted, taste before adding salt)

2 tablespoons plain yogurt

1 tablespoon lemon juice

1 tablespoon finely chopped shallots

1 tablespoon finely chopped cilantro

½–¾ teaspoon cayenne pepper

¼ teaspoon salt

1 teaspoon olive or canola oil

1 teaspoon whole sesame seeds

Put the peanut butter, 1 tablespoon water, yogurt, lemon juice, shallots, cilantro, cayenne, and salt in a small bowl and mix until smooth. Taste for balance of seasonings. Put the oil in a small, heavy frying pan and set on medium heat. When hot, put in the sesame seeds. Shake until the sesame seeds either brown slightly or begin to pop. Lift up the pan and add the sesame seeds and oil to the chutney. Stir to mix.

Yogurt Sambol with Tomato and Shallot

This yogurt relish comes from the Tamil communities of Sri Lanka and is called Curd Sambol. It may be served with most South Asian meals. It may also be eaten at lunch as a salad.

SERVES 4

1 cup plain yogurt
¼–½ teaspoon salt
Freshly ground black pepper
⅛–¼ teaspoon cayenne pepper
1 medium tomato, cut into small dice
1 medium shallot, peeled and chopped
    finely

1 tablespoon olive or canola oil
¼ teaspoon whole brown mustard
    seeds
8–10 fresh curry leaves or 4 fresh basil
    leaves

Put the yogurt in a bowl. Mix gently with a whisk or fork until smooth and creamy. Add the salt, pepper, cayenne, tomatoes, and shallots and mix again.

Pour the oil into a very small pan and set over medium-high heat. When hot, put in the mustard seeds. As soon as they start to pop, a matter of seconds, add the curry leaves and then quickly lift up the pan and empty its contents into the bowl of yogurt. Mix.

Sweet-Sour Yogurt wth Apple and Shallot

Yogurt relishes are eaten with meals throughout India. They are nearly always savory, though in western states like Gujarat a little sugar is added as well as the salt to give a sweet-sour-salty flavor.

SERVES 4–6

1¼ cups plain yogurt
¼–½ teaspoon salt
Freshly ground black pepper
⅛–¼ teaspoon cayenne pepper
1 teaspoon sugar
¼ teaspoon finely grated peeled fresh
    ginger

½ medium Granny Smith apple,
    peeled, cored, and coarsely grated
2 tablespoons olive or canola oil
¼ teaspoon whole cumin seeds
1 small shallot, peeled and cut into fine
    slivers

Put the yogurt in a bowl. Beat lightly with a whisk or a fork until smooth and creamy. Add the salt, pepper, cayenne, sugar, ginger, and apple. Stir to mix.

Pour the oil into a very small pan or small frying pan and set over medium-high heat. When hot, put in the cumin seeds. Let them sizzle for 10 seconds and add the shallots. Stir and fry on medium heat until the slivers just start to turn brown at the edges. Empty the contents of the pan, including the oil, into the yogurt mixture. Stir to mix.

Yogurt Relish with Okra

This is a simple and delicious relish to serve at Indian meals.

2 tablespoons olive or canola oil
$\frac{1}{4}$ teaspoon whole brown or yellow
    mustard seeds
12 medium-sized fresh okra, tops and
    tips removed and cut crossways
    into $\frac{1}{3}$-inch slices

Salt
1 cup plain yogurt
$\frac{1}{8}$ teaspoon cayenne pepper, or to taste

Pour the oil into a small frying pan and set over medium-high heat. When hot, put in the mustard seeds. As soon as they start to pop, a matter of seconds, add the okra. Stir for a minute. Now turn the heat down to medium low. Stir and fry for 8–10 minutes or until the okra is lightly browned. Sprinkle $\frac{1}{8}$ teaspoon salt over the okra, mix, and take the pan off the heat. Set aside.

Put the yogurt in a bowl. Whisk lightly with a fork until creamy. Add $\frac{1}{4}$ teaspoon salt and the cayenne. Stir to mix.

Just before eating, fold the entire contents of the frying pan into the yogurt.

Yogurt with Pineapple

Something between a relish and a curry, this may be served with most Indian meals.

SERVES 4

2 cups fresh pineapple cut into ½-inch cubes
2 tablespoons sugar
3 tablespoons finely grated coconut (use the frozen kind or use desiccated coconut, page 283)
1 cup plain yogurt
1¼–1½ teaspoons salt
1 fresh hot green chili (such as bird's-eye), finely chopped

1 tablespoon olive or canola oil
½ teaspoon whole brown mustard seeds
¼ teaspoon whole cumin seeds
2 hot dried red chilies
10 fresh curry leaves or 6 fresh basil leaves
2 tablespoons finely sliced shallots or onions cut into fine half rings

Put the pineapple, sugar, and ½ cup water in a pan and bring to a simmer. Stir and cook over low heat until the liquid evaporates, about 10 minutes. Add the coconut and stir once or twice. Take off the heat and set aside to cool.

Put the yogurt in a bowl and beat lightly with a fork or whisk until smooth and creamy. Add the salt, green chili, and cooled pineapple-coconut mix. Stir to mix.

Put the oil in a small frying pan and set over medium-high heat. When hot, scatter in the mustard seeds, cumin seeds, and red chilies. As soon as the mustard seeds start to pop, a matter of seconds, add the curry leaves and shallots. Turn heat to medium. Stir and cook until the shallots start to brown. Now pour all the contents of the frying pan into the bowl of pineapple yogurt and stir it in.

Yogurt Relish with Spinach

Any soft green, such as chard leaves, may be substituted for the spinach here.

2 tablespoons olive or canola oil
¼ teaspoon whole brown or yellow
    mustard seeds
½ clove garlic, sliced
5–6 ounces fresh spinach leaves,
    chopped

Salt
1 cup plain yogurt
⅛ teaspoon cayenne pepper, or to taste

Pour the oil into a small frying pan and set over medium-high heat. When hot, put in the mustard seeds. As soon as they start to pop, a matter of seconds, put in the garlic. Cook and stir for a few seconds. Add the spinach and stir for about 5 minutes or until the spinach is just cooked through. Add about ¼ teaspoon salt and mix it in.

Put the yogurt in a bowl. Whisk lightly with a fork until creamy. Add ¼ teaspoon salt and the cayenne. Stir to mix.

Just before eating, fold the entire contents of the frying pan into the yogurt.

Yogurt with Tomatoes and Chickpeas

Here is an easy everyday yogurt relish. I like to use a good whole-milk yogurt here, but if you prefer a low-fat variety it would work well too. My cherry tomatoes were on the larger side so I cut each into eight portions. Use more if they are smaller and just quarter them. Serve with most Indian meals or eat by itself as a snack.

SERVES 3–4

1¼ cups plain yogurt
¼ teaspoon salt, or to taste
Freshly ground black pepper
1 tablespoon very finely chopped red
    onions or shallots
1 cup drained cooked chickpeas
    (canned are fine, organic canned
    are best)

About 3 large cherry tomatoes, cut into
    8 pieces each
1 tablespoon chopped cilantro
1/16–¼ teaspoon cayenne pepper

Put the yogurt in a bowl. Beat lightly with a whisk or fork until smooth. Add all the other ingredients. Stir to mix. Adjust seasonings as needed.

Zucchini Yogurt

This is a typical Gujarati dish: slightly sweet, slightly salty, slightly hot, and dotted with mustard seeds. I just love it. In India it would be served with a meal, but if you are in the habit of having a yogurt for lunch, try this very nutritious version.

SERVES 4

2 cups coarsely grated zucchini (10 ounces zucchini)

1¼ cups plain yogurt

¾ teaspoon salt

1 teaspoon sugar

Freshly ground black pepper

⅛ teaspoon cayenne pepper, or to taste

2 teaspoons canola or olive oil

½ teaspoon whole brown or yellow mustard seeds

2 fresh bird's-eye chilies, slit partially, or 3 long slivers cut from a jalapeño pepper

8 fresh curry leaves, or 4 fresh basil leaves, torn up

Put the grated zucchini into a small pot along with ¼ cup water. Bring to a boil, cover, turn heat to low, and simmer 2 minutes. Empty into a sieve to drain and then refresh by letting cold water run over it. Squeeze out as much of the water as you can.

Put the yogurt in a bowl. Add the salt, sugar, pepper, and cayenne. Beat with a fork or whisk until smooth and creamy. Add the drained zucchini and mix well.

Put the oil into a small pot and set over medium-high heat. When hot, put in the mustard seeds and, as soon as they pop, a matter of seconds, the chilies and curry or basil leaves. Take the pot off the heat quickly and pour its contents over the yogurt. Stir to mix in.

Darshini Cooray's Sri Lankan Mustard Paste

Here is a condiment that I just cannot live without. You can add a dollop to curries or use it as you might any prepared mustard. It perks up hot dogs, my husband smears it on bacon and ham, it goes with roast beef, and it is a lovely, pungent addition to sandwiches. We always keep a jar in the refrigerator. Try smearing it on fresh pineapple slices to serve with a curry meal or a ham or pork roast (see next recipe), or use it to make Vegetable Pickle (see page 258).

MAKES 1 CUP

6 tablespoons whole brown or yellow mustard seeds
3 large cloves garlic, finely chopped
One 1½-inch piece fresh ginger, peeled and finely chopped
1 cup apple cider vinegar or red wine vinegar plus a little more, as needed

3 teaspoons cayenne pepper
3½ teaspoons salt
¼ teaspoon ground turmeric
4 teaspoons sugar

Mix the mustard seeds, garlic, ginger, and vinegar together in a bowl. Cover and leave overnight. Empty the contents of the bowl into a blender and blend until you have a paste. If the blender is sluggish or the paste too thick, add another 2–3 teaspoons of vinegar. The density of the paste should be that of Dijon mustard. Add the cayenne, salt, turmeric, and sugar. Whir once to mix and taste for balance of seasonings. Put in a jar and leave, unrefrigerated, for 3 days to mellow. The paste may now be refrigerated and used as is or to make pickles and relishes.

Pineapple Relish with Mustard Paste

Nose-tingling and refreshing, this Sri Lankan relish goes well with all curry meals. You could also serve it at Western meals with roast pork or pork chops.

SERVES 6

2¼ cups peeled and diced fresh pineapple

3 tablespoons Sri Lankan Mustard Paste made according to the preceding recipe

Put the pineapple in a bowl. Add the paste and stir to mix.

Vegetable Pickle with Sri Lankan Mustard Paste

When I first ate this Sri Lankan pickle, known simply as Sin-ghala Achcharu, it was made with green beans and carrots, but it may be made with other vegetables as well, including green papaya, found in East Asian and South Asian markets, and cauliflower. You may combine all these vegetables if you like, cutting each of them so the pieces are more or less the same size.

MAKES 3 CUPS

2 tablespoons salt

6 ounces green beans, trimmed and cut crossways into ¾-inch pieces

3 medium carrots, trimmed, peeled, and cut into about the same size pieces as the beans

Sri Lankan Mustard Paste made according to the recipe on page 256

Pour 8 cups of water in a pan and bring to a rolling boil. Add the salt and the green beans. Boil for 30 seconds and add the carrots. Boil for 30 seconds and quickly drain the vegetables. Shake out all the water and put the vegetables in a bowl. Add the mustard paste and mix. Put the vegetables in a jar and leave to mature in the refrigerator for 3 days.

ABOUT LASSI

Lassi, *which is a Punjabi word now adopted by much of North India and the world, is a yogurt drink. It may be made out of yogurt thinned out with water—or milk, as they do in the Punjab, where they like their drink tall and rich—or it can be made out of real buttermilk, which is what is left when thinned-out yogurt is churned and the butter is removed.*

In India, lassis *may be had at breakfast, lunch, or as a day-time snack. In North India, they tend to be quite simple: salty or sweet. The salty ones are seasoned with just salt and perhaps some ground roasted cumin, and the sweet ones are flavored with sugar and perhaps some cardamom. In the south, the yogurt drinks tend to have mustard seeds, curry leaves, red chilies, ginger, and even cilantro. They are often poured over rice, though they may be drunk as well. These days all manner of inventive* lassis *are served everywhere, with all kinds of fruit and seasoning in them, from mangoes to bananas and guavas. Feel free to improvise. You may use whole-milk yogurt (I like proper Greek yogurt or acidophilus yogurt best) or skim-milk yogurt, whatever you prefer.*

Yogurt Lassi with Seasonings

I like to refrigerate this *lassi,* covered, with all the seasonings in it, for a couple of hours. Then I strain and serve it. It is particularly good at the very start of a meal, served in tiny glasses to whet the appetite. (You may also strain and serve it as soon as it is made, with a couple of ice cubes. The flavors will be mellower.) You can easily double or triple the recipe.

MAKES 1½ CUPS AND SERVES 1 AS A LONG DRINK AND
2–3 AS SMALL APPETIZER DRINKS

1 cup plain yogurt (preferably Greek or
    acidophilus yogurt)
½ teaspoon salt
½–1 fresh hot green chili (such as
    bird's-eye)

7–8 fresh curry leaves or 2–3 fresh
    basil leaves
One ⅓-inch slice fresh ginger, peeled
    and chopped
1 tablespoon chopped cilantro

Put all the ingredients as well as ½ cup water in a blender and blend for 2–3 minutes. Strain and serve.

Sweet Yogurt Lassi

MAKES 1½ CUPS AND SERVES 1 AS A LONG DRINK AND
2–3 AS SMALL APPETIZER DRINKS

1 cup plain yogurt (preferably Greek or
acidophilus yogurt)

1 tablespoon extra-fine sugar
4 cardamom pods

Put all the ingredients along with ½ cup cold water into a blender. Blend for 2 minutes. Strain and serve as is or with a couple of ice cubes, if desired.

Sweet Mango Lassi

This is best made when good fresh mangoes are in season. When they are not, very good-quality canned pulp from India's excellent Alphonso mangoes may be used instead. Most Indian grocers sell this.

SERVES 2

1 cup plain yogurt (preferably Greek or acidophilus yogurt)
1 cup chopped peeled ripe mango (canned Alphonso slices or pulp may be substituted)

4 cardamom pods
2 tablespoons extra-fine sugar

Put all the ingredients plus ½ cup cold water into a blender and blend for 2 minutes.

Check for desired sweetness, adding more sugar if needed. Strain and serve as is or with a couple of ice cubes.

Easy Masala Chai (Spiced Tea)

At all of India's roadside stalls, Masala *Chai* is served already sweetened. I have added about 1 teaspoon sugar per cup in this recipe, which makes the tea just mildly sweet. You may double that amount, if you prefer.

SERVES 4

$\frac{1}{16}$ teaspoon cinnamon powder
$\frac{1}{16}$ teaspoon clove powder
$\frac{1}{16}$ teaspoon cardamom powder (if you do not have it, throw in 4 cardamom pods)
$\frac{1}{16}$ teaspoon ginger powder

4–5 generous grinds of the pepper grinder
3 tea bags of good, unflavored black tea (I use PG Tips)
2 cups whole milk
4 teaspoons sugar

Put 3 cups water in a pan. Add the cinnamon, clove, cardamom, ginger, pepper, and tea bags. Bring to a boil. Cover, turn heat to very, very low, and simmer gently for 10 minutes. Add the milk and sugar. Stir and bring to a simmer. Pour through a fine strainer and serve.

Desserts

In much of India, Pakistan, Bangladesh, and Sri Lanka, fresh, seasonal fruits are served at the end of family meals. In those parts of India where whole meals—from soup to nuts, as it were—are served in one go on individual *thali*s (very large, rimmed metal plates, each holding at least half a dozen small metal bowls), something sweet is often placed on the *thali*. This could be as simple as a sweetened yogurt.

We actually have two kinds of sweets. There are sweet-meats—little rounds, diamonds, lozenges, and cookie shapes, often made with nuts or nuts and long-cooked milk, or flour and *ghee,* or flour and coconut milk, some in syrup and some not—that are made by specialists known generally as *halvai*s (halva makers) in North India. Mostly, we just buy these from the market and have them with tea or, in some communities, at the end of a meal.

Then there are the pudding-like dishes—*kheer* in the north, *payasam* in the south—usually consisting of milk cooked slowly with grains or *dal*s, that are made at home for special occasions. In the villages, they might be the highlight of a harvest celebration; in the cities, they might conclude a birthday dinner.

The ancient, holy city of Varanasi in North India has been in continuous existence for 3,000 years. There is a narrow lane there that goes off a street where pickles, chutneys, uten-sils, and other food-related fare are sold. This lane is very, very narrow. A high wall runs along one side; on the other is a row of small, open stalls, each just big enough for a couple of shallow, three-foot woks and a man seated beside them.

The woks all contain milk that is being cooked down slowly, sometimes reduced to a solid, dough-like form, and sometimes to a thick cream, to make the hundreds of sweetmeats and desserts that India loves.

Although I had known that the wok probably began its life in India as the *karhai*, I had never quite understood its original purpose until I came to this lane. For India's ancient ancestors, milk and milk products were close to sacred. They were offered to the gods in the form of drinks and sweets and partaken of by the people as God's own food. To make many of these offerings, milk often had to be boiled down in a vessel heavy enough so it would not catch at the bottom and shallow and wide enough to allow for maximum evaporation. The answer was the Indian *karhai,* the shallow, early version used even today as it was 3,000 years ago.

For this chapter, I have picked some desserts that are simple to make. The milk still needs to be boiled down, but the process is made less laborious, sometimes by adding tinned condensed milk (even Indians in India take this shortcut), and by heating up the milk initially in a microwave oven.

For all the milk desserts, use whole milk and find a pan that is very heavy and wide.

Cardamom-Flavored Cream for Fruit

What is required here is not a cream that one can go out and buy. This "cream" is really a kind of pudding or *kheer,* thickened by boiling milk down, not by adding starch to it. In order to take some of the labor out of the process, Indians have taken to adding condensed milk. This works very well indeed.

This is a thinnish cream, ideal to serve with fruit. I put the cut-up fruit (mangoes, guavas, pears, peaches, and bananas are ideal, but I have used berries as well) in individual bowls, or in old-fashioned ice cream cups, and then pour the flavored cream over the top.

MAKES 2 CUPS AND SERVES 4–6

4 cups whole milk
6 cardamom pods

¼ cup sugar
½ cup sweetened condensed milk

Bring the milk to a boil over medium or medium-low heat in a very heavy, wide pan, deep enough to let the milk rise a bit without boiling over. Stir as the milk heats. (I prefer to heat up my milk in a microwave oven and just pour it into the pan to speed up matters.) As soon as the milk starts bubbling, add the cardamom pods and stir. Adjust the heat, generally to medium low, so the milk simmers steadily without boiling over or catching at the bottom. Cook this way, stirring now and then, for about 25 minutes. Stir in any skin that forms. (It tastes very good when cold.) Add the sugar and condensed milk. Stir and cook another 10 minutes. Remove cardamom pods, cover, and cool in the refrigerator.

Rice Pudding or Kheer

This rice pudding is known as *kheer* in North India, Pakistan, and Bangladesh, and eaten under different names throughout South Asia. It consists, in its basic version, of nothing more than milk, cardamom for flavor and aroma, rice, and sugar. In villages and towns, rice harvests are generally celebrated with a *kheer*. In some communities, new husbands and wives feed each other a spoonful of *kheer* during the final part of the wedding ritual. It may be served lukewarm, at room temperature, or cold. Because it is associated with celebration, expensive ingredients are often added, such as saffron, nuts, and dried fruit. Here is the basic version, the one I love the most; you may scatter a tablespoon of chopped pistachios over the top before serving.

SERVES 3

3 tablespoons basmati rice
5 cups whole milk

8 cardamom pods
½ cup sugar

Put the rice in a clean coffee grinder and whir just long enough to break most grains into 2–3 pieces. Some may stay whole. You may also do this in a mortar.

Bring the milk to a boil over medium or medium-low heat in a very heavy, wide pan, deep enough to let the milk rise a bit without boiling over. Stir as the milk heats. (I prefer to heat up my milk in a microwave oven and just pour it into the pan to speed up matters.) As soon as the milk starts bubbling, stir it, adding the rice and cardamom pods. Keep stirring. Adjust the heat, generally to medium low, so the milk simmers steadily without boiling over or catching at the bottom. Cook this way, stirring now and then, for about 40–45 minutes. Stir in any skin that forms. (It tastes very good when cold.) Add the sugar and stir another 2–3 minutes. Take off the heat and pour into a serving dish. Remove the cardamom pods. Allow to cool, stirring now and then so no skin forms on the top. Cover with plastic wrap and refrigerate until needed. (Remember that this pudding may also be served lukewarm or at room temperature.)

Rice Pudding with Saffron and Nuts

This pudding is cooked just like the preceding one but with a few additions.

1 teaspoon saffron threads
1 small sugar cube or $\frac{1}{2}$ teaspoon
    granulated sugar
5 cups whole milk
8 cardamom pods

3 tablespoons basmati rice
$\frac{1}{2}$ cup sugar
2 tablespoons slivered or chopped
    pistachios

Put the saffron and sugar cube in a mortar. Pulverize with the pestle. Add to the milk when you put in the cardamom pods. Cook the rice pudding according to directions in the preceding recipe for 45 minutes. When you are adding the sugar, add most of the nuts, keeping some aside for garnishing the top when the pudding has cooled down a bit.

Tapioca Pearl Kheer

Tapioca pearls and sago pearls are made from two completely different plants, the first from the starchy tapioca/cassava root and the other from the starchy pith removed from the trunk of the sago palm. One originated in the New World, the other in Southeast Asia. Yet the two are endlessly confused. Since their starch is very similar, it hardly matters where cooking is concerned. Indian grocers often put both names, tapioca pearls and *sagudana* or *sabudana* (sago pearls), on the same packet. I grew up with this *kheer,* or pudding. When I came home from school in the middle of a hot afternoon, my mother would have individual terra-cotta bowls of this waiting in the refrigerator. It was very simple and basic, nothing more than milk, sago, cardamom for flavor, and sugar. We called it *sagudanay ki kheer,* or sago pearl pudding, though it may well have been made with tapioca pearls.

SERVES 4

¼ cup tapioca pearls (get the ones that are ⅛ inch in diameter)
5 cups whole milk

8 cardamom pods
4½ tablespoons sugar (or more to taste)

Soak the pearls overnight in water that covers them generously. Drain well the next day and leave in the strainer.

Bring the milk to a boil in a very heavy, medium pan over medium heat. (I actually like to heat the milk in my microwave oven and then pour it into a pan set over medium heat.) Add the pearls and cardamom and stir them in. Adjust the heat so the milk is at a good simmer but does not threaten to boil over, somewhere near medium low. Cook for about 50 minutes, stirring from the bottom every 5 minutes or so. The milk should not catch at the bottom. Add the sugar and stir it in. Cook another 5 minutes. You should now have 3½–4 cups.

Remove the pudding from the heat and allow to cool, stirring every now and then to prevent a skin from forming. Remove and discard the cardamom pods. Put into a serving dish. Cover with plastic wrap, pushing the wrap down so it lies directly on the surface of the pudding. Refrigerate. It will thicken as it cools.

Tapioca Pearl Kheer with Saffron and Nuts

This recipe is very similar to the last, only a bit grander.

SERVES 4

Crush 1 teaspoon saffron threads in a mortar and add them to the milk when you are heating it. When you add the sugar, put in 2 tablespoons golden raisins and 2 tablespoons chopped pistachios as well. Just before serving, sprinkle a tablespoon of very finely chopped pistachios over the top of the pudding.

Vermicelli Kheer

In India and Pakistan a very fine pasta, known as *seviyan,* is used for this quick pudding. Most grocers in the West sell it laid out in long, slim boxes, but in cities like Lahore you can find it in open markets—all exposed, in the shape of little nests of thin pasta piled up into a mountain. The pasta is broken up and lightly browned before it is cooked into a pudding. I find that angel-hair pasta, which often comes in the shape of nests, makes a very good substitute for *seviyan,* and that is what I have started to use. This pudding may be eaten hot, warm, or at room temperature. In Pakistan, it is known as *sheer korma* and in India as *seviyan ki kheer.* On a cold wintry day in North India or Pakistan there is nothing nicer than a warm version of this pudding.

The nuts and raisins are optional. You may leave them out altogether and then, if you like, just sprinkle some chopped almonds or pistachios over the top.

SERVES 4

5 cups whole milk

8 cardamom pods

3 tablespoons butter or *ghee*

3 cups (about 3 ounces) angel-hair pasta, broken up into 1-inch pieces

¼ cup slivered almonds, blanched (optional)

2 tablespoons golden raisins (optional)

½ teaspoon saffron threads (optional)

½–¾ cup sugar

Combine the milk and cardamom and set to heat in the microwave oven or in a heavy pan over medium heat. The milk needs to get close to the boiling point.

Put the butter in a heavy, wide pan and set over medium-low heat. As soon as the butter has melted, put in the pasta and almonds. Stir until just golden. This takes very little time. Pour in the hot milk, stirring as you go. Add the raisins, saffron, and sugar. Bring to a simmer over medium heat. Stir and cook for about 10 minutes or until the pudding has thickened. Serve hot, warm, or at room temperature.

Shrikhand (Yogurt Cream)

This sweet cream, which tastes a bit like crème fraîche, only with a more flowing, creamy texture, is a simple Gujarati dessert, so cooling during Gujarat's hot summer days. In May and June, when mangoes are in season, thick mango puree is folded in. A teaspoon of saffron threads, roasted and soaked in milk, may be added at the same time as the sugar (see method on page 289) or dried fruit (golden raisins, soaked in boiling water for an hour and squeezed), nuts (chopped pistachios or almonds), fresh fruit (chopped mangoes, bananas, berries), and fruit purees.

SERVES 4–6

8 cups plain whole-milk yogurt

Sugar, 1 cup or more, according to taste

Balance a large sieve over a bowl. Cut a doubled-up piece of cheesecloth so it is large enough to be tied into a bundle. Center it in the sieve. Empty the yogurt into the cheesecloth. Bring opposite ends together and tie into as tight a bundle as possible. Put a 2-pound weight on the top. (Sometimes you need to wait until the yogurt has released a little liquid. I usually put a saucer on top of the bundle and then the weight—often a can—on the plate.) Leave for 2 hours. Put the strained yogurt (you should now have about 3 cups) into a bowl. Add 1 cup sugar. Mix well and taste. Add more sugar if you need it. Cover and refrigerate until needed.

Yogurt Custard

This dense, intense yogurt custard is a specialty of Bengal, where it is called *bhapa doi*—steamed custard. Bengalis have quite a sweet tooth, and this is one of the hundreds of sweet things they buy from the market, all set in terra-cotta pots, to have at the end of their meals.

Here is a quick, easy version that I learned from a Bengali friend. It can be eaten by itself or with fruit. You may double the recipe, using a 4-cup dish. The cooking time should be the same.

SERVES 2–3

1 cup plain whole-milk yogurt

1 cup sweetened condensed milk

Preheat oven to 300°F.

Put the yogurt in a bowl. Beat lightly with a whisk until smooth and creamy. Add the condensed milk. Mix it in thoroughly. Pour the mixture into a 2-cup ovenproof dish and cover it, with foil if necessary. Put this dish into a larger ovenproof dish—or a baking pan—that can hold enough water to come halfway up the sides of the smaller dish and act as a bain-marie. Pour very hot water into this second dish and place both dishes in the oven. Bake for 40–45 minutes or until set. Remove from oven. Lift out the smaller dish and allow to cool. Cover and refrigerate until needed.

Yogurt Custard with Banana

This is made in the same way as in the last recipe, only it has a layer of sliced bananas at the top.

SERVES 2–3

All the ingredients in the last recipe
1–2 bananas
$\frac{1}{4}$ teaspoon ground cardamom seeds
    (you can pulverize the seeds in a
    mortar)

$1\frac{1}{2}$ tablespoons brown sugar

Start making the custard the same way as in the preceding recipe. Put in the oven to bake. When the custard is set (after the 40–45 minutes of baking), remove it from the oven. Cut 1–2 bananas into $\frac{1}{8}$-inch rounds and lay these evenly over the custard, overlapping them slightly, if you wish. Combine the ground cardamom and sugar and sprinkle over the top. Bake another 5–7 minutes or, better still, put it briefly under the broiler to caramelize. Cool, cover, and refrigerate until needed.

Spices, Seasonings, Oils, and Special Techniques

In order to make the foods in this book easier to prepare, I have used a somewhat limited palette of spices and seasonings. But as I am writing about Indian and other South Asian food, a fair number of them are still required. Most can be bought from Indian grocers or via the Internet. Store the dried spices, preferably in their whole form, in tightly closed containers in a closed cupboard, away from sunlight. Grind them in a clean coffee grinder or mortar as needed for optimum flavor. You may also store the ones you use the most in spice boxes sold by Indian grocers, consisting of round stainless steel boxes with individual containers inside them. I suggest that you start by getting only the spices that you need for the specific dishes you wish to cook. Add more spices as you need them. Don't overwhelm yourself.

I have also included some techniques in this section. For example, if you want to know how to grate tomatoes, just look in the index under Tomatoes, alphabetically. For grating ginger, look under Ginger.

LEFT: *Fresh Chili Peppers*
(top) *Bird's-Eye;* (bottom) *Cayenne*

ASAFETIDA   This is one of the seasonings that I consider essential, as it goes to the heart of Indian cooking. It is a resin and not much is needed in a recipe. Only a very small amount gives many Indian dishes their earthy, truffle-like flavor and aroma. It is also a digestive and therefore used frequently with *dal*s. Buy the ground version in the smallest size available and keep the container tightly closed.

ATA   See *Chapati* Flour.

BESAN   See chickpea flour.

BLACK PEPPER   Native to India, whole peppercorns are added to rice and meat dishes for a mild peppery-lemony flavor. Ground pepper was once used in large amounts, sometimes several tablespoons in single dish, especially in South India, where it grows. The arrival of chilies from the New World around 1498 AD has changed that usage somewhat, though it still exists. In some South Indian dishes peppercorns are lightly roasted before use to draw out their lemony taste. In rice and meat dishes, they are often used whole. Indians always leave them on the side, just as you would meat bones or a bay leaf. Do not worry about buying the most expensive kind. What you are paying extra for is size and evenness of shape. That hardly matters to me.

CARDAMOM PODS AND SEEDS   Small green pods, the fruit of a ginger-like plant, hold clusters of black, highly aromatic seeds that smell like a combination of camphor, eucalyptus, orange peel, and lemon. Whole pods are put into rice and meat dishes, and ground seeds are the main flavor in *garam masala,* page 285. This versatile spice is the vanilla of India and used in most desserts and sweetmeats. It is also added to spiced tea and sucked as a mouth freshener. Cardamom seeds that have been taken out of their pods are sold separately by Indian grocers. If you cannot get them, take the seeds out of the pods yourself. The most aromatic pods are green in color. White ones sold by supermarkets have been bleached and have less flavor.

When whole cardamom pods are put into dishes, they are not meant to be eaten. As with other large spices such as cinnamon sticks and bay leaves, they are left on the side of the plate, just as bones would be.

CHAPATI FLOUR   Very finely ground whole-wheat flour used to make *chapatis, pooris,* and other Indian flatbreads. Sometimes called *ata,* it is sold by all Indian grocers. Whole-wheat pastry flour may be substituted.

CHICKEN STOCK   Many of my recipes call for chicken stock. These days you can buy this canned, or freshly made, from good grocers and butchers. I tend to collect leftover chicken and bones in my freezer, and when I have enough, I put it all in a pot along with a peeled carrot and a peeled onion, a bay leaf, a little salt, and enough water to cover everything by about 1 inch. I bring this to a boil, skim it, and then let the pot simmer very gently for 2 hours. I strain the stock and put it in the refrigerator. The next day I remove the congealed fat, and it is ready to use.

CHICKPEA FLOUR   Flour made out of dried chickpeas. In Indian shops this is sold as gram flour or *besan.* In specialty stores it is often sold under its French name, *farine de pois chiches.* Store in the refrigerator to discourage bugs.

CHILIES   While Mexico uses dozens of varieties of chilies in its cuisine, India, which was gifted this new spice in the early fifteenth century, uses mostly the cayenne type—though they are rarely as fiery as the cayenne chilies I grow in my American backyard. Indian chilies are thin, thin skinned, and usually 1½–3 inches long. Indian grocery stores sell both the fresh and dried versions of the chilies that are required for my recipes. Chinese grocers also sell the dried ones, as they are the same as those used in Sichuan food.

Fresh hot green chilies: Many of the dishes in this book call for fresh hot green chilies. What should you use? Indian grocery stores sell a long cayenne-type chili and the small, thin bird's-eye chili. Both are fine to use for Indian food. But what if you are not near an Indian grocery? You can get fresh bird's-eye chilies from Thai grocers, but what if you do not have access to them either?

What are found most commonly in American markets are the much larger, thicker-skinned jalapeños and serranos, which are very different but may be used in their fresh form with this proviso: First check if these chilies are hot—cut one in half lengthwise and then cut off a sliver of skin for a taste. If it is not hot, it won't serve any purpose at all. If it is hot, look at the recipe: if it calls for 1 chili, use about ¼ of the jalapeño, about ½ of the serrano, cut lengthways, *with seeds*. Because of the thick skin, it is best to chop up the chili finely, or use slivers if the recipe suggests whole chilies.

It is not always possible to gauge the heat of green chilies correctly, so it is best to start with the smaller amount suggested in the recipe and then add more a little later in the cooking process should you desire it.

Dried hot red chilies: When my recipes call for these, look for exactly the same chili that is used in Sichuan cookery—red, about 2 inches long and ⅓-inch wide. Often they are dropped into very hot oil, which fries the skin and flavors the oil, giving whatever is cooked in it a browned-chili taste.

Cayenne pepper, chili powder: Indians use pure chili powder, unmixed with any other spices. Cayenne pepper is a fine substitute. They also use Kashmiri chilies, either powdered or whole, for a very special reason—they impart a lovely red color to all foods and are not very hot. These special chilies grow in Kashmir and are similar to the chilies used in making paprika. They are almost impossible to get in their whole form in the West, though some shops do sell a ground version that I do not entirely trust because it looks unnaturally red. For dishes where I might have used ground Kashmiri chilies, I substitute a combination of cayenne mixed with paprika.

CILANTRO   This is the parsley of southern Asia. Wash well and use just the leaves and more delicate stems. To store, stick the cilantro bunch in a glass of water like cut flowers and drape a plastic bag over the greenery.

CINNAMON   Used mainly for desserts in the West, cinnamon, often in its "stick" form, is added to many Indian meat and rice dishes for its warm, sweet aroma. Sri Lankans use it even more, as it is one of their cash crops. This inner bark from a laurel-like tree is also an important ingredient in the aromatic mixture *garam masala,* page 285.

CLOVES   The West calls for cloves when making desserts. Indians rarely use cloves in desserts but do use them in rice, legume, and meat dishes and in the spice mixture *garam masala.* Indians carry the pungently aromatic cloves as well as cardamom pods in tiny silver boxes, to use as mouth fresheners when needed. For the same reason, cloves are always part of the betel-leaf paraphernalia that is offered as a digestive at the end of Indian meals.

COCONUT   Some of my recipes call for freshly grated coconut. You can now buy frozen grated coconut in many South and East Asian groceries. Look for the more finely grated kind. You should not be able to see coarse strands. Hack off what you need and keep what you do not need frozen. You may also use unsweetened desiccated coconut. Just barely cover it with hot water and leave for an hour. Two tablespoons of desiccated coconut will yield about 3 tablespoons of a rough equivalent to grated fresh coconut.

Coconut milk: I use the canned variety. Just use a brand

you like and shake the can well before use. What is not used may either be stored in the refrigerator for a week or be frozen.

CORIANDER SEEDS, WHOLE AND GROUND   Coriander seeds are best bought whole and then ground in small quantities, as needed, in a clean coffee grinder or mortar. They are very easy to crush in a mortar. I do it all the time—and the aroma is glorious.

CUMIN SEEDS, WHOLE AND GROUND   These seeds look like caraway seeds, only plumper and lighter in color. You may buy them in their ground form. Unlike ground coriander, their flavor lasts a long time.

To make ground roasted cumin seeds: Put a few tablespoons of seeds in a small cast-iron frying pan over a medium-high flame. Stir and roast for a few minutes, until the seeds are just a shade darker and give off a strong roasted aroma. Cool off a bit and grind in a clean coffee grinder or crush in a mortar. Save what you do not use in a tightly lidded jar. It can be held for several months.

CURRY LEAVES   They have an exotic, sunny, lemony aroma—that is why they are used. Only fresh leaves will do, as the dried ones have no flavor or aroma at all. Look for a local source if you can or find an Internet one. Or try growing a plant in a sunny spot—it is known as *Murraya koenigii,* botanically. I have finally managed to find some plants in New Jersey. Sometimes fresh basil makes an interesting substitute, but it does not work every time. Unless the basil leaves are very small, they should be torn up first.

CURRY POWDER   Curry powders generally contain a blend of spices including cumin, coriander, turmeric, chili powder, fenugreek, and many more. The flavors and potency can vary. Sometimes I like to add a little to a soup or curry, along with other spices. The curry powder I use is sold as Bolst's Curry Powder, and I get the "hot" version.

DALS   Dried beans, split peas, and other legumes are all sold under the common name *dal* in India. I have decided to use this name throughout the book, as it is all encompassing. Sometimes split peas, in very small amounts, can also be used as a seasoning. *Urad dal,* a split pea native to India, is often used that way in South Indian cooking. It provides a nutty flavor. Other split peas, such as yellow split peas, may be substituted.

FENNEL SEEDS   They have an anise flavor and are wonderful with fish and vegetables such as eggplants.

FENUGREEK SEEDS   Dull yellow and squarish, they provide the earthy, musky taste in curry powders. They have a strong, lingering aroma and are frequently added to Indian pickles.

GARAM MASALA   A mixture of aromatic (and generally expensive) spices that according to the ancient Ayurvedic system of medicine are meant to heat the body. This is the only spice mixture that I ask you to make at home and keep in storage. Its aroma is unsurpassed if mixed and ground at home in small quantities. Also, it will not contain cheap "filler" spices, such as coriander seeds, as many commercial mixtures do. I do keep the store-bought mixture in my cupboard as well for use in certain dishes that require less perfume. My recipes will tell you which one to use.

To make *garam masala* at home:

1 tablespoon cardamom seeds (buy the seeds or remove from pods)
1 teaspoon whole cloves
1 teaspoon whole black peppercorns
1 teaspoon whole cumin seeds
$\frac{1}{3}$ of a nutmeg (just hit it with a meat pounder or hammer to break it)
One 3-inch cinnamon stick, broken up

Grind all these in a clean coffee grinder and store in a dark cupboard.

GARLIC   I use a garlic press to get the pulp. It is quick and easy. You may also mash a clove of garlic by placing the flat side of a knife on it and hitting it with your fist.

GHEE   This is clarified butter, made by boiling down a large quantity of butter until all the water in it evaporates and the milk solids turn hard. It is then strained and is called *ghee.* Now it is ready to be used for all kinds of cooking, including deep-frying. You may buy *ghee* from an Indian grocer. You may find that it is made in the Netherlands!

GINGER   I have mainly used fresh ginger here. This rhizome has a sharp, pungent, cleansing taste and is a digestive to boot. It is now said to help with travel sickness as well. When *slices of ginger* are called for, peel a section of the knob and cut thinnish slices, crossways. When *slivers or minute dice* are called for, first cut the ginger into very thin slices. The slices should then be stacked and cut into very fine strips to get the slivers. To get the *dice,* cut the slivers crossways into very fine dice.

When *finely grated ginger* is required, it should first be peeled and then grated on the finest part of a grater so it turns into pulp. A ginger grater or fine microplane are ideal. When a recipe requires that 1 inch of ginger be grated, it is best to keep that piece attached to the large knob. The knob acts

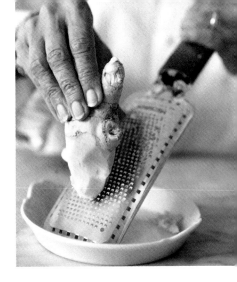

as a handle and saves you from grating your fingers.

Ginger should be stored in a dry, cool place. Many people like to bury it in dry-ish, sandy soil. This way they can break off and retrieve small portions as they need them while the rest of the knob generously keeps growing.

KAFFIR LIME LEAVES   These highly aromatic, lemony, green leaves are sold by Thai grocers. They look like two leaves joined together, top to bottom. The skin of the lime itself is also used in Thai cookery. I was not aware that they were used in South Asian cookery until I went to Bangladesh and smelled that distinct aroma in a *dal.* What leaves you do not use can be frozen. I actually went to New York's Chinatown and bought myself a plant. It is now happily producing limes as well.

LEMON GRASS   There are just a few recipes here where I have used lemon grass. It provides a lemony aroma to Sri Lankan stews and rice dishes. As the grass stalks are tall and hard, you need to cut off and discard the top, leaving about 6 inches of the bottom. Then hit the bulbous bottom end with a hammer to crush it lightly. Now the stalk is ready to go into a pot of stew or a rice dish.

MUSTARD SEEDS, BROWN   India has mustard seeds of all colors, the pale yellow, the black and the brown. The brown are indigenous and most used. All mustard seeds have two distinct characteristics: if they are thrown into very hot oil, they pop and turn nutty; if they are ground, they turn pungent and slightly bitter. In South Asia, they are used in both ways. As they can roll around easily, I grind them in a clean coffee grinder. If you cannot find brown seeds, you may substitute the yellow variety.

NIGELLA SEEDS (KALONJI) This is the black, tear-shaped seed you might have seen on top of some Indian flatbreads such as *naan*s. I love their oregano-like aroma. They are used in Bengal and through much of North India for pickling, for cooking vegetables like eggplants, and for fish curries.

NUTMEG The seed of a round, pear-like fruit, the slightly camphorous nutmeg is used in the making of the aromatic spice mixture known as *garam masala.* To break the nut into smaller pieces, just tap it lightly with a mallet or hammer or meat pounder.

OILS I have usually used plain olive (not extra virgin) and canola oil in this book just to keep the choices manageable, but you can use corn or peanut oil just as easily. For special dishes from Bengal or Kashmir, I use mustard oil.

ONIONS A medium onion is approximately 5 ounces. There are two kinds of onions commonly used in India: the shallot in most of the south and Sri Lanka, and a smallish, pink onion in the north. Indeed, in North India, the word for our onion is *pyaz* and the name for the color pink is *pyazi.*

PAPPADOMS These fine wafers are generally made out of a split-pea dough and dried in the sun. Indian grocers sell them plain or studded with black pepper or cumin or green chilies, or garlic or red chilies—the choices are many. When buying them, make sure that they are pliable, and therefore fresh. Keep them well sealed. They can be deep-fried for a few seconds in hot oil, or roasted over a fire or cooked in a microwave oven for 40–50 seconds.

PAPRIKA Kashmir, India's northernmost state, produces a chili powder that is rather like paprika. It is mild and gives off a lovely red color. To get the same effect, I often combine cayenne pepper with paprika, making sure that the paprika is fresh and still has good color.

SAFFRON I have only used "leaf" saffron (whole saffron threads) in this book. Known in ancient Greece and Rome as well as in ancient Persia and India, this valued spice consists of the whole, dried stigma of a special autumn crocus. Look for a reliable source for your saffron, as it is very expensive and there can be a great deal of adulteration. Indians often roast the saffron threads lightly in a cast-iron frying pan before soaking them in a tablespoon or two of hot milk to bring out the color. This milk is then poured over rice to give it its orange highlights. In Iran, the saffron is pounded with a cube of sugar and allowed to soak in a mixture of melted butter before it is used. This also brings out its color. In much of European cookery a very light pinch of saffron is thrown directly into broths to make risottos and soups.

TOMATOES A medium tomato is approximately 5 ounces. My recipes often call for grated tomatoes. This is the quickest way to get a rough tomato sauce. Grating them does include the seeds, but I have never understood why we throw them away. However, it does get rid of the skin, which can be unsightly in a sauce. I have never seen tomatoes grated anywhere except in India. Here is how you go about it: Use the coarsest side of a grater. I like the four-sided grater that has one whole coarse side. When you start grating, the tomato may refuse to oblige and slip around. Press hard, or even cut off a thin slice on that side, and keep going. When you get to the end, flatten your palm and grate off as much as possible until only the skin is left. Discard the skin. One medium tomato yields

about ½ cup of fresh sauce. To make your own tomato puree, see the box on page 38.

TURMERIC   A rhizome-like ginger, only with smaller, more delicate "fingers," fresh turmeric is quite orange inside. When dried, it turns bright yellow. It is this musky yellow powder that gives some Indian dishes a yellowish cast. As it is cheap and is also considered to be an antiseptic, it is used freely in the cooking of legumes and vegetables. Its color can stain, so use with care.

Index

A NOTE ABOUT THE AUTHOR

Madhur Jaffrey is the author of numerous previous cookbooks, including the classic *An Invitation to Indian Cooking, Madhur Jaffrey's World-of-the-East Vegetarian Cooking,* and *Madhur Jaffrey's Taste of the Far East,* which was voted Best International Cookbook and Book of the Year for 1993 by the James Beard Foundation. She is also an award-winning actress with numerous major motion pictures to her credit. In 2006 her memoir, *Climbing the Mango Trees,* was published. She and her husband live in New York City and in Colombia County, New York.

A NOTE ON THE TYPE

This book was set in Celeste, a typeface created in 1994 by the designer Chris Burke. He describes it as a modern, humanistic face having less contrast between thick and thin strokes than other modern types such as Bodoni, Didot, and Walbaum. Tempered by some old-style traits and with a contemporary, slightly modular letter-spacing, Celeste is highly readable and especially adapted for current digital printing processes which render an increasingly exacting letterform.

Composed by North Market Street Graphics
Lancaster, Pennsylvania

Printed and bound by C&C Offset Printing
Shenzhen, China

Designed by Soonyoung Kwon